THE NELSON A. ROCKEFELLER COLLECTION

MASTERPIECES OF MODERN ART

THE
NELSON A. ROCKEFELLER
COLLECTION

MASTERPIECES OF MODERN ART

Photographs by Lee Boltin
Text by William S. Lieberman
Introduction by Nelson A. Rockefeller
Essay by Alfred H. Barr, Jr.
Edited and with a Preface by Dorothy Canning Miller

HUDSON HILLS PRESS　　NEW YORK

PUBLISHER'S NOTE

The Nelson A. Rockefeller Collection: Masterpieces of Modern Art was originally scheduled to be published in fall 1979. By the end of 1978, texts had been written by Nelson Rockefeller, Alfred H. Barr, Jr., and Dorothy C. Miller, almost all the works of art had been photographed, and editorial and design work were well underway. Rockefeller himself was deeply and enthusiastically involved with the preparation of the book, right up to and including the day of his death.

After Rockefeller's death, the project was temporarily shelved during a period of uncertainty about his various projects. After a time, however, those who had been associated with him on the project came to feel that completion of the book was necessary not only as a memorial to Rockefeller but also as a record of a landmark collection—a record that became all the more valuable for the fact that the collection it documented had effectively ceased to exist. We are delighted to present this publication at this time—in a form that we hope would have pleased Nelson Rockefeller.

The text written by Rockefeller has been left intact, while those by Alfred H. Barr, Jr., and Dorothy C. Miller have been slightly amended to reflect the changed circumstances.

Further, we have been fortunate to be able to add a major essay by William S. Lieberman, adapted from his text for the 1969 Museum of Modern Art catalogue of the Rockefeller collection. We are immensely grateful to Mr. Lieberman, a longtime colleague of Mr. Rockefeller at the Museum, and to the Museum itself, for its kind assistance with this material.

Those works of art that left the collection before Nelson Rockefeller's death are credited to their most recent owners as of December 1978. Those works that were bequeathed to The Museum of Modern Art are credited accordingly in the following pages. A substantial number of paintings and sculpture in and around Mr. Rockefeller's residence at Pocantico Hills in Tarrytown, New York, were bequeathed to the National Trust for Historic Preservation (and are indicated in the captions that follow with the initials NHT). Since Rockefeller's death, his estate has disposed of a number of works; where possible, we have credited the current owners.

HUDSON HILLS PRESS
Paul Anbinder
Lee Boltin

First Edition

©1981 The Nelson Rockefeller Collection, Inc.
William S. Lieberman text © 1969, 1981 The Museum of Modern Art

Published in the United States by Hudson Hills Press, Inc.
    Suite 4323, 30 Rockefeller Plaza, New York, N.Y. 10112

Editor and Publisher: *Paul Anbinder*
Copy-editor: *Harriet Schoenholz Bee*
Designer: *James Wageman; Jos. Trautwein/The Bentwood Studio*
Composition: *U.S. Lithograph, Inc.*
Manufactured in Italy by Amilcare Pizzi S.p.A.

Library of Congress Cataloguing in Publication Data
Boltin, Lee.
    The Nelson A. Rockefeller Collection.

    Bibliography: p.
    Includes index.
    1. Art, Modern—20th century—Catalogs.   2. Rocke-
feller, Nelson A. (Nelson Aldrich), 1908–1979—Art collections—Catalogs.   I. Lieberman, William Slattery,
1924–   .   II. Miller, Dorothy Canning, 1904—
III. Title.
N6488.5.R6B6   709'.04'0074014   81-6752
ISBN 0-933920-24-5   AACR2

Overleaf
Sculpture in the gardens at Pocantico Hills. The works of art, all bronzes, from left to right, are: *Seated Nude*, by Henri Matisse; *Natura Extensa*, by Peter Chinni; and *The Call of the Earth*, by Georg Kolbe.

This book is dedicated to Abby Aldrich Rockefeller,
whose life touched and inspired so many people—
I was one of them!

ACKNOWLEDGMENTS

I am especially indebted to four people for the endless joy I have found in the collecting of modern art in all forms during the past fifty years.

First, my mother, Abby Aldrich Rockefeller, who as much as anyone I know was in tune with her times and had a zest and love of life and beauty in all its forms. Mother deeply believed that art not only enriches the spirit but also, as she put it herself, "makes one more sane and sympathetic, more observant and understanding. . . ." I have tried to emulate her positive, creative response to people and to the excitement of the rapidly changing scene in which we live.

Second, Wallace K. Harrison, the person who, next to my mother, had the greatest impact on my life in terms of understanding the relation between the cultural creations of our times and the environment from which they spring. We were closely associated during this entire period, both in connection with The Museum of Modern Art and in innumerable other projects. From him I learned that if one helps to create an atmosphere of beauty, serenity, and peace, it nourishes the spirit and fosters dignity and love in those embraced by it. From his greatness as a human being and his sensitivity and strength as an architect, I gained insight into how we can positively relate to and harmonize with the forces that surround us. In the architectural projects we worked on together, both large and small, we always focused on the enhancement of human values through the use of form and space, combined to the greatest possible extent with nature and the creative arts.

Third, Alfred H. Barr, Jr., to whom I owe so much, whose innovative perception and understanding of humanity and the great creative periods of history made him intensely aware of the significance of our own times. The depth of his scholarly background, combined with his extraordinary sensitivity, made it possible for him to identify the great contemporary artists and their works as they created them. Time has proven his judgment to be virtually infallible. For almost thirty years, in close collaboration with the trustees of The Museum of Modern Art, he built the Museum collection and organized a series of exhibitions that catapulted modern art into center stage in this country and abroad. Thus was built one of the most significant cultural institutions of our time. Through the Museum, the great art of the period became a vibrant symbol of the culture from which it derived its inspiration. Through my own close association with Alfred over three decades, I was constantly enlightened, inspired, and amazed by the genius of this gentle maestro—this "high priest of modern art"—who is revered and respected throughout the world.

Fourth, Dorothy C. Miller, to whom I am infinitely indebted and grateful. Dorothy is an extraordinary person, with a very rare insight in the area of contemporary art. She was Alfred's closest associate and collaborator in discovering new artists and identifying their best works, and in writing and editing many of the Museum's innumerable scholarly publications. Dorothy has never received the recognition due her for the importance of her role at the Museum and in helping the public appreciate modern art.

Dorothy has worked with me over a long period, selected the objects from the collection for the book, and organized them in a meaningful way. My joy in making the collection and in sharing it with you through this book is importantly due to her.

Nelson A. Rockefeller
October 1978

The Enclosed Garden at Pocantico Hills, including
sculpture by Reg Butler, Robert Adams, Gaston Lachaise,
Aristide Maillol, Elie Nadelman, Ezra Orion, Jean Arp,
Henri Matisse, Peter Chinni, Georg Kolbe, Fritz Wotruba,
and David Smith.

CONTENTS

LIST OF ILLUSTRATIONS

Colorplates are preceded by a bullet (•)

PREFACE

by Dorothy Canning Miller

Those of us who have had a part in working with Nelson Rockefeller's collection of modern art have found it a stimulating experience. Nelson showed us what it means to possess a true passion for collecting—many kinds of art, from various parts of the world and periods of time. His interests were broad—and the appetite omnivorous.

From the start, Nelson's collection of modern art was one of the most adventurous in private hands. His open mind and his immediate inner response to new work, whether for it or against, enabled him to "see" what he was looking at and to make quick decisions which for him were valid. He refused to buy anything simply because the artist was famous or represented some phase of contemporary art which would enrich his collection. His guide always had to be his own feeling.

In the 1940s and '50s, during the middle years of forming the collection, contemporary art in America greatly extended its boundaries, both in the mediums it used and in the subjects it chose. Pioneering works in a great variety of new materials and with new concepts of space, which were only later to be readily accepted, at first seemed strange and dissonant to many in the art world, including collectors. But Nelson looked with eager interest at everything and never seemed to suffer from the prejudices that afflicted so many. He did not have to be urged to accept experiment in the visual arts as part of the current scene.

The splendid paintings and sculptures which ornamented Nelson's country house and its surrounding landscape, his New York apartment, his house in Maine, a house in Washington, and the Executive Mansion in Albany were not acquired simply to decorate those residences. He lived with works of art, perhaps more closely than anyone I have known. He loved to rearrange whole rooms full of paintings and drawings, and he did this work himself. Trying the large outdoor sculptures in ever new locations also gave him much pleasure. He constantly used these objects for relaxation and spiritual nourishment.

Before he became deeply involved in the world of politics as governor of New York in 1959, Nelson visited the art galleries regularly and bought from them. He went to the shows of new art organized periodically at The Museum of Modern Art and bought from them. And through the years, no matter how busy, he always gave several concentrated Sunday hours to studying questions relating to his collection, along with the new art books and countless catalogues from here and abroad.

He also spotted interesting and unusual works of art in his travels. A perfect case in point was Picasso's *The Bathers*, which he first saw on his official visit to Expo '67 in Canada. It was the central piece in the outdoor sculpture exhibition. Nelson noticed in the catalogue that it was on loan from a Paris art gallery, so he wired the gallery the next day and acquired this important work.

During the early 1970s, changes began to be made in the content of the collection. Nelson had always intended that it be fluid, like the collection of The Museum of Modern Art, which was early described as having "somewhat the same permanence a river has—continuous but gradually changing in content. This metabolic process is of special value because it makes sure that the collection will not be simply a cumulative repository. . . ." Perhaps this purpose remained in Nelson's mind from his days as a very young trustee of the Museum. In any case, a number of works left his collection from time to time, sometimes given to museums or to members of his family, sometimes sold to make space available for new works, or to facilitate the acquisition of monumental sculpture—which continued to be one of Nelson's major interests until his death in January 1979.

This book was first planned soon after the collection's first major exhibition, *Twentieth-Century Art from the Nelson Aldrich Rockefeller Collection*, which I organized for The Museum of Modern Art in 1969. The catalogue of that exhibition lists the 221 works which were shown and illustrates 132, including some large sculptures which could not be moved from Pocantico Hills to the Museum. Also illustrated are several of the great paintings which were destroyed by fire in the Executive Mansion in Albany in 1961. Like the collection itself, the exhibition was divided about evenly between paintings and sculptures, and it also contained drawings, prints, and illustrated books.

For the present book, which does not include illustrated books or prints, a selection of key items was made from the Rockefeller collection of several thousand works of modern art, ultimately reducing the number to more than 250 covered here, including many acquired in the 1970s. Since the Rockefeller collection was such a significant document in the field of modern art, it was felt all along that the reference value of this book would be enhanced by the inclusion of some works which—by gift or sale—had left the collection over the years. With the group of capital paintings and sculptures bequeathed to The Museum of Modern Art since Nelson Rockefeller's death joining the masterworks he generously donated during his lifetime, treating the collection as a historic entity takes on even greater significance.

A sequence of large plates was created to illustrate, almost entirely in color, most of the works chosen, arranged in roughly chronological order. Within this sequence, works by the same artist or relating to a particular art movement were grouped together. Additional works not included in this main sequence of plates are illustrated in the principal texts by Alfred H. Barr, Jr., and William S. Lieberman.

I hope this book will provide a lasting record of Nelson Rockefeller's involvement with the heroic period of twentieth-century art. He started acquiring major works by its pioneers at a time when few American collectors had got around to them. It took flair and imagination to build a great collection of modern art at that time. He followed the initial acquisitions with a brisk and sympathetic approach to contemporary art, both here and abroad. His collecting may, I believe, be considered a historic episode in the development of American taste.

INTRODUCTION
by Nelson A. Rockefeller

If one loves beautiful things and is in tune with the life and culture of one's own time, the most natural fulfillment is to collect contemporary art that reflects the period. Art is the symbol of the culture to which it belongs. Thus every culture should have its own style of art.

This was particularly true of the art of the Western world as it developed during the first half of the twentieth century. Artists had been freed from the rigid framework of realism by the revolutionary breakthrough of Post-Impressionism at the end of the nineteenth century. Thus freed, they developed, in rapid succession, a series of radically new forms of expression that reflected the vitality of a changing world.

To understand the great art of that period as it unfolded, one has to view that art as an organism with its own soul, its own forms of expression, and its own convictions that were intimately related to the time in which it was created.

In the early part of our century, only a limited number of people on either side of the Atlantic were aware of the significance and magnitude of the changes that were taking place in the cultural life of our times.

While the creative innovations of the late nineteenth and early twentieth centuries were made first by European artists whose names are now so familiar to all of us, it was avant-garde Americans who led the way in appreciating and collecting their works. In New York, a small group of such collectors recognized the tremendous importance of the brewing cultural revolution and were terribly excited by it. My mother, Abby Aldrich Rockefeller, was one of them. She had acquired a taste for the arts from her father, Senator Nelson W. Aldrich of Rhode Island. He collected extensively in Europe, especially the Mediterranean countries, and he took her along on his collecting trips when she was a young girl.

After my mother married, she collected on her own—beautiful things she loved from various periods. She was a free spirit who loved people and all aspects of life. Her collecting was a reflection of these qualities. She collected primitive art, oriental sculpture, Japanese prints, American folk art and, finally, modern European and American art. Her taste was eclectic, spontaneous, and almost infallible.

Abby Aldrich Rockefeller's art gallery on the top floor of her home at 10 West 54th Street, designed by Donald Deskey. The works of art include paintings and drawings by Vincent van Gogh, Charles Sheeler, Peter Blume, Odilon Redon, and Joseph Whiting Stock. The cast-aluminum table and upholstery fabric reflect the overall Art Deco design of the gallery.

My father, John D. Rockefeller, Jr., was also a collector, but much more a connoisseur in the traditional sense—of early Roman and Gothic sculpture, medieval tapestries, and finely painted Chinese porcelains of the Ming, early Ch'ing, and other periods.

Although Mother's interests in art were not shared by Father, in the early 1920s he agreed to the converting of an upstairs floor of our house at 10 West 54th Street into a gallery by the brilliant modern designer-architect, Donald Deskey.

As children we grew up surrounded by the spectrum of diverse cultures, which became part of the life we lived and absorbed. It was my rare privilege and good fortune to be close to my mother during this exciting period and thus to share her intellectual curiosity and boundless aesthetic enthusiasm for new forms of creative expression—a joyous way of life that has never left me. We visited art galleries together and I listened to her discussions with her friends.

During winter 1928–29, while Mother was vacationing in Egypt, she met, quite by chance, her friend Lillie P. Bliss. Miss Bliss, about ten years older than Mother, was the daughter of a successful textile manufacturer. Under the influence of the painter Arthur B. Davies and the famous 1913 Armory Show, which he had helped organize, she had been an avid collector and advocate of the highly controversial art then appearing on the scene. In Egypt together, Mother and Miss Bliss exchanged ideas on establishing a new museum in New York to house what was considered to be their outlandish hobby.

Later, on shipboard while returning from Egypt, Mother met Mrs. Cornelius J. Sullivan, the former Mary Quinn, a one-time Indiana farm girl who had had a successful career as a teacher of art in New York and London before she married Mr. Sullivan, a prominent New York attorney and collector of modern art. Mary Quinn Sullivan, it developed, was an old friend of Lillie Bliss. More importantly, she saw eye-to-eye with Mother and Miss Bliss on the need for creating a museum of modern art, since established museums had not yet perceived the significance of the modern movement. Even the great Metropolitan Museum of Art wanted no part of modern art, though Miss Bliss had pressured the Met into holding one exhibition of Impressionist and Post-Impressionist works in 1921.

Therefore, Mother and her friends agreed that the only way to cut through the barriers of tradition and timidity was to establish a new museum, one that could act as a catalyst in crystalizing public awareness and appreciation of these contemporary creative forces, these new forms of expression.

In late May 1929, the three women had a meeting with A. Conger Goodyear at our house to discuss the formation of a museum of modern art. Goodyear, a very interesting and independent spirit, had been president of the Albright Gallery in Buffalo, where he was a successful businessman. He also had avant-garde taste, and had acquired for himself a very good collection of Post-Impressionist painting. While in Paris, he had bought a beautiful Picasso of the Rose period, La Toilette, for the Albright Gallery. The trustees were so upset by the painting that, at the next board meeting when he happened to be out of town, they voted him out as president of the museum. Mr. Goodyear was so indignant that he not only resigned from the Albright's board, but also left Buffalo and came to New York City to live.

Obviously, he was exactly the person the three women were looking for to be president of the new museum—a man of independent and discriminating taste, fearless, and deeply committed to modern art.

It was a perfect combination. The three women among them had the resources, the tact, and the knowledge of contemporary art that the situation required. More to the point, they had the courage to advocate the cause of the modern movement in the face of widespread division, ignorance, and a dark suspicion that the whole business was some sort of Bolshevik plot.

Within twenty-four hours of their first meeting with Goodyear, he had accepted the presidency of the new museum. By November 1929, The Museum of Modern Art was in business at the Heckscher Building, Fifth Avenue at 57th Street, opening with a loan exhibition of works by Cézanne, Gauguin, Seurat, and van Gogh.

Mother used to illustrate the need for the new museum by citing the tragedy of Vincent van Gogh, one of the great pioneers of Post-Impressionism, who had died at age thirty-seven in an institution for the destitute, unable even to sell his paintings to buy bread, only to have the greatness of his work recognized years after his death. Mother's objective for the new museum was to reduce dramatically the time lag between the artist's creation of and the public's appreciation of great works of art.

This required of the new museum an ability to seek out and identify important new works of art as they were being created—without the benefit of time to test their intrinsic worth. The Museum of Modern Art did just that and thus played a unique role in our society. This was made possible by the basic concept and the dedication of those who organized the Museum and, most importantly, by the brilliant young art historian, Alfred H. Barr, Jr., who became its first director.

At the time of the founding of the Museum, my mother and the other trustees decided to establish a Junior Advisory Committee of young people who were active in art programs at various colleges. The group they selected included Edward M. M. Warburg and Lincoln Kirstein, who were leaders in the arts at Harvard, Monroe Wheeler, Philip Johnson, Elizabeth Bliss (now Eliza Parkinson), and me.

We started meeting regularly in Mother's gallery, Alfred Barr joining us when he could. He wasn't very much older than we were, although he was already recognized widely as an art scholar. He inspired us, opened our eyes, and broadened our understanding of contemporary developments in the world of art and their relation to the evolving society in which we lived.

Many of us on the Junior Advisory Committee became trustees of the Museum, involved in all aspects of the Museum's activities, not only in the fields of painting and sculpture, but in architecture and design as well. This intimate involvement had a great impact on all of us. For me, the whole experience was tremendously stimulating.

I had gone on the Board of Trustees of the Museum in 1932, then became its treasurer. And when the Museum's new building on West 53rd Street was completed in 1939, and A. Conger Goodyear resigned as president, after piloting the Museum so successfully during its first decade, I was elected to succeed him as president. I was thirty years old.

The presidency got me more involved with the Museum's program of acquisitions, its permanent collection, its exhibitions and circulating exhibitions, and the develop-

Henri Matisse. *La Poésie* (Mural for Fireplace). 1938.
Oil on canvas. c. 111 × 72 inches (282 × 182.9 cm).
Private collection.

Fernand Léger. Mural for Fireplace. 1939.
Oil on canvas. c. 111 × 72 inches (282 × 182.9 cm).
Private collection.

Marc Chagall. "A Nelson Rockefeller en bon souvenir
—Marc Chagall Venee 1950." 1950.
Watercolor and pen and ink on paper.
15 × 22⅛ inches (38.1 × 56.2 cm).

ment of new departments of prints, industrial design, films, and photography. It also brought me into increasingly intimate contact with artists and creative leaders in a wide range of cultural fields.

Thus, when I had purchased a new apartment in 1936, I decided to decorate it in the modern style. I worked with Wallace K. Harrison, my close friend and a brilliant architect, who designed very simple wood panelling with a Louis XIV influence in order to provide a warm and inviting background. We asked Jean-Michel Frank, one of the outstanding French designers of the period, to design the interior. He commissioned distinguished young artists to do the furnishings, including the lamps and tapestries for the rugs and chair coverings. These artists included the Giacometti brothers, Alberto and Diego, and Christian Bérard.

Wally designed two fireplaces in the living room with space for great murals around them, and our friends Henri Matisse and Fernand Léger accepted commissions to undertake the murals. Matisse did the mural in Paris from full-scale drawings of the fireplace, but Léger came over to New York and actually did the painting in the apartment.

I used to watch Léger with fascination as he painted and the details of the mural unfolded. After he had finished, we liked it so much that we persuaded him to do additional murals for the circular stairwell and the hallways, both upstairs and down. Léger was a wonderful human being, and we remained friends until his death.

I was constantly working with artists on commissions for various projects. Thus, modern art for me was not only the most rewarding aesthetic experience, but also a warm personal experience because of my friendships with artists.

Often I have bought works of art directly from artists while visiting their studios both in this country and abroad. These were always fascinating experiences. I remember making a visit with Alfred Barr to Georges Mathieu's Paris studio, where I purchased one of his paintings. He had a unique style, and I remember commenting on the great feeling of depth which I felt in this particular painting. He was indignant because he said that, quite to the contrary, his paintings had no depth—which only goes to show that

in nonrepresentational art every person can interpret and enjoy a painting as he or she sees it.

There was another delightful visit, during that same trip, to Jean Arp's studio in the country outside Paris. I bought a concrete cast of one of his beautifully sculptured forms for the garden.

On occasion, artists who were friends and whose work I collected would give me an inscribed painting or drawing or a small piece of sculpture. These especially treasured works bring back very happy memories of associations with Chagall, Miró, Léger, Lipchitz, and others.

One of the happiest personal associations began in 1946 when I was president of The Museum of Modern Art and we gave Henry Moore the first one-man show in the garden of the new Museum building. Our early friendship has lasted over the years. Years later, while I was governor in Albany and could not get to see the New York exhibitions, I wrote him a note saying that I felt out of touch with his more recent work and asking him to recommend a few major pieces, since I wanted to bring my Moore collection up to date. He was delighted and wrote back recommending two—*Atom Piece* and *Knife Edge Two Piece*—both of which he sold me directly from his studio in England. They are thrilling works and have become two of my favorites.

I had started collecting modern art in the early 1930s, shortly after I got out of college. Obviously, I had been influenced by the long exposure to my mother's taste and enthusiasm, the impact heightened by the excitement of working with the newly formed Museum through the Junior Advisory Committee.

Like Mother's, my taste was eclectic. While painting and sculpture of the modern era appealed to me most because of its strength both in form and color, I had also from the very beginning collected prints, drawings, and watercolors. In addition, during the 1940s and '50s, I made rather an extensive collection of books, mostly published in Paris, illustrated by such great contemporary artists as Picasso, Matisse, Braque, Chagall, Maillol, and Miró.

Among the modern American artists I collected early were Edward Hopper, Charles Burchfield, Max Weber, George "Pop" Hart, Maurice Prendergast, Gaston Lachaise, Jules Pascin, and Yasuo Kuniyoshi. They were all friends of my mother; I had grown up with and admired their work. As new artists kept emerging, I would start collecting their works—for example, Alexander Calder, Jacques Lipchitz, and Louise Nevelson, getting me more and more into sculpture.

At the same time, my mother and I followed the extraordinary art movement that was developing in Mexico and Latin America under the leadership of such great painters as Diego Rivera, José Clemente Orozco, and David Alfaro Siqueiros.

I must say, however, that I was always most strongly drawn to the work of the great European pioneers of modern art, for example, Henri Matisse, Juan Gris, Pablo Picasso, Alexey Jawlensky, and Wassily Kandinsky. Their strength in terms of composition and color was overwhelming.

Of all of them, Picasso was always my favorite. His restless vitality and constant search for powerful new forms of expression, combined with his superb craftsmanship and sense of color and composition, have remained an unending source of joy and satisfaction to me. I continued to

Pablo Picasso. *Guernica* (Tapestry, 1955, after a maquette of the painting of 1937). Wool. 120 × 264 inches (314.8 × 670.1 cm).

collect all forms of Picasso's works throughout the 1930s, '40s, and into the '50s—until the prices of his work went out of sight. It was at this point that I first got the idea of having great works of art reproduced. There were at least two dozen of his greatest paintings in museums or other private collections that I particularly admired. One of these was his famous Spanish Civil War painting, *Guernica*, which I knew well, as it had long been on loan to The Museum of Modern Art. I learned from Wally Harrison that a huge tapestry of this painting had been made from a maquette which Picasso had designed after the original painting. The artist himself had chosen the colors of the yarns and supervised the weaving. When I saw the tapestry, I bought it immediately.

Alfred Barr was disturbed by my purchase of what he had heard was just a distorted copy of one of the greatest paintings of the twentieth century; shades of yellow and brown had been introduced into the tapestry, whereas the original had been painted exclusively in stark blacks, grays, and whites. However, when Alfred actually saw the tapestry for the first time, he completely changed his mind. He realized that Picasso had created a totally new work of art, designed to be woven as a tapestry. The subject had been sensitively and brilliantly adapted to the different medium, and the result was a stunningly beautiful work of art in its own right.

This gave me the courage to communicate with Picasso through an old friend of his, Madame Marie Cuttoli, to see if he would be interested in doing a series of maquettes of some of his other great paintings from which tapestries could be woven under his supervision. To my great surprise, he was enthusiastic about the idea and accepted it as a new challenge. Thus he and I started a project that continued until his death some twenty years later in 1973.

Pablo Picasso. *Girl with a Mandolin (Fanny Tellier)* (Tapestry, 1972–75, after a maquette of the painting of 1910). Silk. 118 × 86½ inches (299.7 × 219.7 cm).

Nelson Rockefeller's art gallery at Seal Harbor, Maine, designed by Philip Johnson. The works of art include paintings and sculpture by Adolph Gottlieb, Frederick J. Kiesler, Philip Guston, Ernest Briggs, Alberto Giacometti, Fritz Bultman, and Alexander Calder.

Each year Picasso would design a maquette after another of the great paintings I loved, would choose the colors of the yarns and supervise the weaving of the tapestry. He insisted on determining the size of each tapestry, which he invariably made much larger than the original painting. The result was that I acquired over the years some twenty tapestries by Picasso after his greatest paintings, among them *Les Demoiselles d'Avignon*, 1907; *Girl with a Mandolin (Fanny Tellier)*, 1910; *Pitcher and Bowl of Fruit*, 1931; *Girls with a Toy Boat*, 1937; and *Night Fishing at Antibes*, 1939. They were all limited to editions of one or three.

During the two decades I was working with Picasso, I was also collecting examples of the new schools of art that were appearing on the scene, products of the dynamic modern movement in all its broad sweep. Abstract Expressionism, which grew partly out of Surrealism, yet was often nonrepresentational in style, was one of the strongest and most comprehensive, encompassing a large number of the American artists who had emerged during the 1940s and '50s.

In the 1960s and '70s, I became more and more interested in monumental modern sculpture—almost to the exclusion of paintings and graphics. The gardens at the family home in Pocantico Hills slowly became a virtual outdoor sculpture gallery. Starting with the marble copies of classical works which had been collected by my grandfather and

father, I added sculptures by Matisse, Picasso, Maillol, Moore, Calder, Lipchitz, Lachaise, Nadelman, David Smith, and many others.

I had always been very fond of Sandy Calder as a person and was fascinated by the creative originality of his mobiles and stabiles. In the early 1930s, I had purchased a small stabile, *Spiny*, which I especially loved. After I became involved with large outdoor sculpture, it occurred to me one day that Sandy might be interested in making a huge replica of the little *Spiny*. So I talked with him about it and he liked the idea. The next summer he took the original to his Paris foundry and made a new version more than twelve feet high. It is stunning—and it has been tremendously admired as it stands majestically on a hill overlooking the Hudson River.

Thus has my collection unfolded over fifty years, comprising the works of artists I have admired, works in which I have found infinite pleasure.

I had only one problem, and that was the lack of space for the paintings and sculpture. So, in the 1950s I worked with Philip Johnson on designing and building a gallery in an old coal wharf close to our home in Maine. It worked out beautifully and helped for awhile to solve the space problem, as did my transformation of the Executive Mansion in Albany into a virtual modern art gallery in 1959. Then, in the early 1960s, I converted into galleries the long corridors in the basement of my grandfather's house in

Pocantico Hills (they had originally been built to support the garden terraces). With an ingenious lighting system worked out by Mr. Johnson, these proved to be a great success.

When I left Albany in 1973 I had to put a great deal of art into storage. However, I never liked to keep art for long where it could not be enjoyed, so some works have been given to museums and others have been sold.

Twentieth-century art has been a vital part of my life; in fact, it has become a way of life for me. It has given meaning and value, perspective, and fulfillment to my life, as well as constant joy. It is a current that has run deep and strong in me regardless of the pressures, turmoil, and responsibilities with which I have lived and worked.

Art has always been a source of faith and hope, of inspiration to people throughout the world. It is a bridge between peoples everywhere who otherwise have little contact—and often less understanding and trust. I cannot conceive of a nobler pursuit.

Nelson Rockefeller's underground art gallery at Pocantico Hills, designed by Philip Johnson. The works of art include paintings, sculpture, and tapestries by Elie Nadelman, Fernand Léger, Aldo Calo, Pablo Picasso, Louise Kruger, Gottfried Honegger, Andy Warhol, and Amadeo Gabino.

A room in the underground art gallery at Pocantico Hills, photographed in 1981. The works of art partially or fully visible on the walls include paintings, sculpture, and prints by Edgar Negret, Fritz Glarner, Louise Nevelson, Charles Davis, Luis Perelman, Salvador Soria, Elie Nadelman, Reinhoud, Pablo Picasso, Max Ernst, Ludvik Durchanek, Jorge Eielson, Mary Bauermeister, and Julio Alpuy. Sculptures on the table are by Marisol, Tomio Miki, and Henry Moore.

ON NELSON ROCKEFELLER AND MODERN ART

by Alfred H. Barr, Jr.

As I think of Nelson Rockefeller's lifelong involvement with art I find myself remembering that I once remarked: "Nelson needs art more than any man I know. Works of art give him a deep, almost therapeutic delight and refreshment. Yet beyond his private satisfaction there lies a strong desire to share his treasures with others." This is the keynote not only of what he collected for himself, but of his undaunted insistence on making art available to others, an idea that ran like a gold thread through the manifold absorbing activities of his private and public life. As art was a necessity to him, he felt that it was a necessity for all people, and he made it his task to provide it—with courage, persuasiveness, and generosity.

Exposed since childhood to traditional works of art of the highest quality, Nelson was gently steered by his mother, Abby Aldrich Rockefeller, to an appreciation of contemporary art. She herself had developed a predilection for it so marked that she was probably the most crucial of the three initial founders of The Museum of Modern Art, which opened early in November 1929, soon after the stock market crash.

Not many months after, the trustees realized that it was important to gather around the Museum a body of younger people who would feel an involvement in it and, if possible, share some of its responsibilities. This group was known at first as the Junior Advisory Committee and included Elizabeth Bliss (now Eliza Parkinson), Philip Johnson, Lincoln Kirstein, James Johnson Sweeney, Edward M. M. Warburg, and other amateurs and potential collectors. Nelson Rockefeller joined the committee in 1930, later became its chairman, and in 1932 was elected a trustee of the Museum. He was twenty-four years old.

At this time there was great enthusiasm for the many frescoes that had blossomed in Mexico after the long revolution. Abby Aldrich Rockefeller had bought three large paintings and a 1927 sketchbook of forty-five watercolors of May Day in Moscow by the most renowned of the Mexican painters—Diego Rivera. The Museum was much interested in the artist, and it seemed highly desirable to have an exhibition of his work. Accordingly, a large show was held in winter 1931–32; it included six big frescoes painted in New York expressly for the exhibition, three on Mexico and three on New York subjects.

The fame of the Mexican murals and the serious interest of many New York artists led Nelson Rockefeller and the Junior Advisory Committee to sponsor the exhibition *Murals by American Painters and Photographers*. Lincoln Kirstein was put in charge, selected thirty-five painters, and commissioned from each a small study for a triptych and

one of the three panels in full size. The exhibition opened on May 3, 1932. The Depression was at its worst, and many of the artists had leanings toward the political left; as a result half a dozen of the commissioned paintings were attacks on capitalism, notably William Gropper's painting, *Class Struggle in America Since the War*, which featured a not-too-happy portrait of J. P. Morgan. The young Nelson Rockefeller bravely visited the famous financier, who graciously forgave.

Some members of the public were shocked by the show, the trustees embarrassed, and members of the Junior Advisory Committee somewhat shaken, all the more so since several of the murals were not of high quality. As chairman of the committee, Nelson took much of the responsibility for the exhibition. He stepped into the trouble and had occasion to show for the first time in public his diplomatic talent as well as his liberal attitude and his concern for artists.

By 1932, some of the buildings of Rockefeller Center were approaching completion. John D. Rockefeller, Jr., as well as Mrs. Rockefeller and Nelson were agreed that imposing murals by painters of world fame should adorn the entrance hall of 30 Rockefeller Plaza, the largest of the skyscrapers. Picasso, solicited by the architect Raymond Hood, refused. Matisse, though a warm friend of Mrs. Rockefeller, was working on his mural for the Barnes Foundation and was unwilling to start on another project. In May 1932, Diego Rivera also refused; he had several reasons, and, in any case, he was working on his great Detroit commission. Nevertheless, Nelson persisted. As Bertram D. Wolfe wrote in his book, *Diego Rivera, His Life and Times*:

> Again and again relations were strained in these lengthy negotiations between the obstinate architect and the no less obstinate painter, but always it was Nelson Rockefeller, functioning as diplomat, friendly intervener, executive vice-president of Rockefeller Center, Inc., and real boss of the whole undertaking, who finally straightened things out and sustained Rivera in his various demands as a painter.

In November 1932, Rivera said yes, but various arguments followed until March 1933, when he left Detroit for New York, thanks to Nelson, and finally began painting at Rockefeller Center. Nelson was delighted. But very serious trouble ensued because of the aggressively political iconography of the fresco. In his friendly but firm letter of May 3, 1933, to Rivera, Nelson wrote: "As much as I dislike to do so I am afraid we must ask you to substitute the face of

Fernand Léger. Mural for Circular Stairwell. 1939–41.
Oil on canvas.
Sculpture at left is *Torso*, a cast-stone figure by Wilhelm Lehmbruck.

The Abby Aldrich Rockefeller
Sculpture Garden,
The Museum of Modern Art,
New York, 1953.
Designed by Philip Johnson.

Fritz Glarner. Mural for Dining Room Walls and Ceiling. 1964.
Oil on canvas. Room size: 30 × 15 feet.

some unknown man where Lenin's face now appears. . . .''

Rivera answered amicably, but said no. Rivera and Nelson both lost; in 1934 the mural was destroyed.

In 1939–40, Nelson Rockefeller and Wallace K. Harrison undertook to commission another mural for Rockefeller Center. Their friend, Fernand Léger, who had made his first movie in 1924, was delighted at the prospect of decorating the entrance hall of the International Building with a "cinematic mural": images to be shown as an animated film on the wall facing the escalators in the hall. "There is poetry in the machine age of America," Léger said, and he called New York "the greatest spectacle on earth."

For this commission Léger painted a number of watercolors as studies for the main motifs of the moving pictures, all compositions inspired by recurrent fragments of the New York scene: skyscrapers with lighted windows, tugboats, U.S. flags, and the Statue of Liberty. But this cinematic mural, though devoid of the political connotations of Rivera, did not come to fruition either. The authorities in charge of Rockefeller Center were against it.

A lesser man than Nelson Rockefeller would have been daunted by the frustrations of the Rivera and Léger murals, but he continued to commission works of art, though for his own use. In 1938, he asked Matisse to paint an overmantel for the large sitting room of his New York apartment. A year later Léger decorated another fireplace for the same room and painted the wall of a spiral staircase. In 1964 Fritz Glarner produced abstract paintings completely covering the walls and ceiling of the dining room. All these

assignments were difficult, because of unusual shapes and locations; however, all were highly successful.

Perhaps the most important private commission that Nelson undertook—this one on behalf of his family—was the rose window in memory of his mother for the Union Church of Pocantico Hills. The window was to be placed over the chancel. After considerable time and thought Nelson decided to ask Matisse to design the window, even though the master was already very old and ailing. Nelson requested from the first that it should be quite abstract; a long correspondence ensued and Matisse sent a preliminary maquette which was not entirely satisfying.

On October 28, 1954, Matisse wrote, in a letter which arrived on November 1, that he was nearing final completion of the design. Nelson was elated, but early in the morning of November 3 the announcement of Matisse's death came over the radio. We were shocked, then concerned about the future of the window, but later on the same day a letter, perhaps his last, dated November 1, arrived from Matisse. It opened with this sentence: "Thanks to the design of the last full-size maquette I have been able to bring to a happy conclusion the work I had undertaken. . . .''

Henri Matisse and Abby Aldrich Rockefeller were fond of each other. In 1956, when the memorial window was dedicated and the ceremony over, one of the sons remarked, "Nothing would have pleased Mother more."

Abby Aldrich Rockefeller set for Nelson many precedents of generosity toward the collection of The Museum of

Modern Art. In 1935 she gave the Museum's first fund for the purchase of works of art and, in 1938, a much larger fund for the same purpose, a gift in which Nelson joined. She also gave most of her own collection of modern paintings in 1935, her sculpture in 1939, a large collection of prints in 1940. In 1942 Nelson granted the Museum an Inter-American Fund, which he renewed whenever needed over a period of twenty-five years; as a result, the Museum was able to acquire probably the most important collection of Central and South American modern painting. He also made possible the Abby Aldrich Rockefeller Sculpture Garden for the Museum—a masterpiece of Philip Johnson's design. All these gifts of Nelson's were made anonymously.

In 1958 Nelson Rockefeller selected some sixteen of his best works of art to be given eventually to the Museum. Eleven years later, at the opening of an exhibition of over two hundred items from his collection, he added to his promised gifts, bringing the total, in 1969, to twenty-five; included were most of his choicest paintings and a number of his sculptures. These are works that admirably complement the collection of the Museum.

Among them are several Picassos, all excellent in quality, some of them famous: the *Girl with a Mandolin (Fanny Tellier)*, 1910, perhaps the best known early Cubist work; the 1916 painting, *Still Life: "Job,"* and a collage, *Guitar*, 1913, both Cubist; a splendid still life, *Pitcher and Bowl of Fruit*, 1931; *Interior with a Girl Drawing*, a great work of

the mid-1930s; and *The Striped Bodice*, 1943, a portrait of Dora Maar. Braque is represented by *Clarinet*, 1913, a superb collage. Admirable are Gris's *Guitar, Bottle, and Glass* and *The Sideboard*; Léger's classic *Woman with a Book*; Matisse's *View of Collioure and the Sea*, 1911, exceptional in color, and a rare lithograph, *Odalisque in Striped Pantaloons*. The Futurist Boccioni's triptych *States of Mind* is renowned, as is de Chirico's *The Song of Love*, so admired by the Surrealists. Two paintings by Klee, *Fear* and *Heroic Strokes of the Bow*, are affectingly vehement. The sculptures are Lehmbruck's elegant *Dancer*; *Reclining Figure*, 1934, by Gonzalez, master of wrought iron; Gabo's Euclidean *Construction in Space, X*; and Calder's small *Spiny*, 1942, so intense that Nelson commissioned an outdoor version six times higher, suggesting a faraway procession of giraffes.

Two of the greatest paintings of our century's first decade are the "Douanier" Rousseau's *The Dream* and Matisse's *Dance* (First Version). Both masterpieces were painted almost at the same time and both were offered to the Museum by dealers during the Depression when there were, unfortunately, virtually no purchase funds available. By coincidence the paintings were then acquired privately by two members of the Museum's Advisory Committee. Twenty years later, one of them, Sidney Janis, needed to sell *The Dream* in order to start his gallery on 57th Street; and in 1963 Walter P. Chrysler, Jr., decided to sell *Dance*

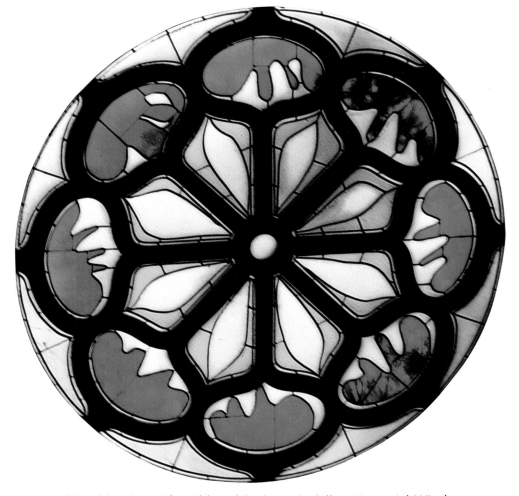

Henri Matisse. The Abby Aldrich Rockefeller Memorial Window,
Union Church of Pocantico Hills, New York. 1954.
Stained glass with lead mullions. 76 inches (193 cm) diameter.

23

Henri Matisse. *Odalisque in Striped Pantaloons*. 1925.
Lithograph. 21 × 17¼ inches (53.3 × 43.8 cm).
The Museum of Modern Art, New York. Nelson A.
Rockefeller Bequest.

(First Version) to make it possible to open his own museum
in Provincetown. Both, as a courtesy, offered these very
important pictures to the Museum because of their early
connection with it.

In 1953, when *The Dream* came up for sale, the Museum again lacked funds; several of the trustees and other
friends of the Museum, one after another, were offered the
picture but were not favorably inclined; and to make matters worse there was a deadline to be met and another
museum competing. As a last resort there was nothing to
do but to cable Nelson Rockefeller who, as it happened,
was in Africa. On his way back, he cabled from Athens:
"Think Museum should purchase Rousseau. We will work
out payment somehow. Nothing I can do this year. Nelson." Less than a year later, he gave *The Dream* to the
Museum as a very handsome birthday present for its
Twenty-fifth Anniversary. Then, in the spring of 1963, as
a grand surprise, Nelson Rockefeller gave the Museum
Matisse's *Dance* (First Version).*

In 1939, Nelson Rockefeller had been elected president
of The Museum of Modern Art. A year later he was appointed Coordinator of Inter-American Affairs under President Roosevelt for four years. By this time Nelson was a

man of considerable experience and was fully aware of the
fact that most civilized countries—other than the United
States—systematically organized all manner of cultural exchanges and exhibitions as a subtle yet powerful means of
propaganda; the activities of the excellent British Council
were an example.

Nelson was convinced that it would be a good plan to
send the American Ballet Caravan to Latin America. It was
"the first [American] government-sponsored performing arts
program abroad." He also arranged, through The Museum of
Modern Art, to send an extensive exhibition of contemporary American painting to Latin America, enlisting the help
of five leading museum directors to make the selections.
He brought the catalogue of the show before the chairman
of a congressional committee, hoping to secure funds for a
series of such exhibitions, but this legislator exclaimed
indignantly, "You are spending the taxpayers' money in
sending this material to South America?" Nelson answered,
"Well, Congressman, I'm sure you don't set yourself up
as a judge in the field of art, and neither do I. But the
purpose of this show is to explain ourselves to the people of
the Western Hemisphere, the other American republics.
They feel that we are a people whose sole interest is in
money and power, and they are not familiar with our
cultural forms of expression. And this is very important in
terms of developing understanding. And [this art] you may
not like, I may not like. But this is what the directors of the
five greatest museums in the United States say is the best
contemporary form of cultural expression. And this is what
we are sending down." Nelson won by persuasion: *La
Pintura Contemporánea Norteamericana* traveled to Buenos Aires, Montevideo, and Rio de Janeiro.

During the Eisenhower period of the early 1950s, Nelson
Rockefeller, as Under Secretary of Health, Education, and
Welfare, worked with Secretary Oveta Culp Hobby in persuading the president to sponsor a bill for a national council on the arts. The president sent the bill to a senator with a
request that he introduce it on the floor, but the latter
unfortunately dubbed it "The Free Piano Lesson Bill." The
bill never got off the ground.

All through his life Nelson surrounded himself with works
of art, many works of art. They were a great love, a source
of happiness and recreation; he could not live without
them. Accordingly, when he was elected governor of New
York and established residence in the Executive Mansion,
he sent to Albany a large selection of paintings, sculptures,
and drawings from his collection. Such things had never
been seen before in Albany, and it took singular boldness
to confront the state legislators with such strange and daring works.

On December 31, 1958, only a few hours were available between the departure of the outgoing Governor Harriman and Nelson Rockefeller's first grand dinner party. He
had asked Dorothy Miller, curator at The Museum of Modern Art, to help hang the pictures and place the sculptures.
When she arrived, she found some eighty works hastily
stacked all over the first floor along with television sets,
luggage, and other things which had arrived from New
York the day before. Within an hour, and minutes before
Nelson himself arrived, she had a tentative plan ready for
his approval, without which she could not go into action

because he always liked to arrange his collection himself, so personal was his involvement. He threw off his jacket at once, refused all telephone calls, and spent the next three hours, his first in Albany, working on the installation. Every available wall space was used, and furniture, mantel ornaments, lamps, and plants were banished in order to make more room for art. Members of the family and their guests began arriving and were pressed into service to help finish the show and finally to stow away the leftovers in closets upstairs.

On New Year's Day, after the inauguration, hundreds of official guests attended the formal reception in the Executive Mansion. They found the Victorian house newly embellished with splendid works by Matisse, Picasso, Klee, Tobey, Feininger, Noguchi, Nadelman, and many others. A few months later the governor's remarkable group of American Abstract Expressionist paintings, including works by Pollock, Gorky, Tomlin, Kline, Brooks, Gottlieb, and Guston, arrived in Albany after a year's tour of Europe as part of The Museum of Modern Art exhibition *The New American Painting*.

It is hard to tell whether Nelson had foreseen that the collection with which he instinctively surrounded himself would eventually gain converts and bear results most favorable to the cause of modern art. But what he hoped and what happened is best told in his own words in "The Arts and the Quality of Life," a chapter in his book, *Our Environment Can Be Saved*, published in 1970:

Well, it was a new experience for Albany and for the legislators. They had never seen anything like it. . . . But the exciting and interesting development was to

The small sitting room at the Executive Mansion in Albany. Works of art include paintings and sculpture by Georges Braque, Pablo Picasso, Paul Klee, Lynn Chadwick, and Elie Nadelman.

Henri Rousseau. *The Dream.* 1910.
Oil on canvas. 80½ × 117½ inches (204.5 × 298.5 cm).
The Museum of Modern Art, New York. Gift of Nelson A. Rockefeller.

come. The legislators came to the Executive Mansion, with their wives, and little by little, they got used to the art. Soon they would come to see if there was anything new in the house. We had a list printed which they could take home, containing the names of the artists and pertinent data. . . .

As Governor of New York, I tried again to get legislative support of the arts. This time I was able to do better. I discovered that while I could never carry a tune, sometimes I could persuade a legislature. Thus in 1960, my second year as Governor, a New York State Council on the Arts was enacted by the legislature at my request. This was the first organization of its kind to be created either at the state or federal level—and all 49 other states and the federal government itself eventually followed our lead.

In the mid-1960s, the New York legislature authorized the construction of a monumental new complex of state office buildings in Albany, a concept on which Rockefeller and Wallace K. Harrison had been working for over a year. The project called for a great library and cultural center, a state convention center, and two small theaters in addition to eight office buildings. The complex is a fitting center for the governmental and cultural activities of the Empire State, and just beginning to be appreciated.

A fraction of one percent of the construction cost of the Empire State Plaza or South Mall project, as it was originally known,* was dedicated to the acquisition of the works of contemporary New York State artists—paintings, murals, and monumental sculpture for the gardens. Rockefeller appointed a small committee under the chairmanship of Harrison to select the artists. Seymour Knox, president of the Albright-Knox Art Gallery in Buffalo and chairman of the New York State Council on the Arts, and René d'Harnoncourt, director of The Museum of Modern Art, were the other members. After René's tragic death in 1968, Dorothy Miller took his place.

Thanks to their knowledge, taste, and dedication, the collection today—about one hundred paintings and sculptures in and around these fourteen buildings in Albany—represents at their best a decade of the leading painters and sculptors of New York State—a unique monument to its cultural vitality.

*Editor's note: In 1978, it was officially renamed The Governor Nelson A. Rockefeller Empire State Plaza.

Henri Matisse. *Dance* (First Version). 1909.
Oil on canvas. 102½ × 153½ inches (259.7 × 390.1 cm).
The Museum of Modern Art, New York. Gift of Nelson A. Rockefeller in honor of Alfred H. Barr, Jr.

THE NELSON A. ROCKEFELLER COLLECTION

by William S. Lieberman

In May 1939, Nelson Aldrich Rockefeller answered several questions about himself and art in the course of a radio interview:

"I'm interested in art that relates to life in our own day, that expresses the spirit of our time—art that isn't cloistered and set apart, art that includes the house and the motor car . . . as well as painting and sculpture. . . . The true enjoyment of art is more than a vague and dutiful respect paid to the traditions of the past. At home, when we put a picture on the wall, I'm not so much interested in its historical value. I'm more interested in the pleasure it gives—the contribution it makes to the room and to the house. . . . What attracts me most about the art of our time is its vitality—the way it explores new possibilities and makes use of new materials. . . . I think it's important that all forms of art reach the public—it's important that we know all about the flourishing arts of our own day."

In answer to a final question, "Do you enjoy having a share in this work?" he replied, "To be frank, I get a great kick out of it."

A profound respect for present-day concerns and the pursuit of broad visions, many of which seemed audacious at the time of their conception, are two of the great strengths that have characterized the family of John D. Rockefeller, Jr., over three generations, producing extraordinary results, both public and private. One such flowering was the collection of modern art owned by Nelson Aldrich Rockefeller.

Although it should be kept in mind that Nelson Rockefeller's collection was personal and not systematic, and although he might have acknowledged the ensuing classifications with surprise, his collection of twentieth-century art can be grouped into five major categories: Cubism and Futurism; Expressionism; Surrealism; American painting; and sculpture. His choice of European painting and sculpture of the first half of this century reveals three definite preferences: masterworks by the innovators of Cubism and Futurism; Expressionism, defined in terms sufficiently broad and personal as to include Matisse and Modigliani; and Surrealism in sculpture, and its affinities in painting before and after the 1920s.

In American painting, Nelson Rockefeller's preferences were more contemporary; for the most part, the examples were purchased soon after they were painted. These acquisitions demonstrated a particular commitment to the Abstract Expressionists who were painting in New York during the late 1940s and '50s. His preferences in American sculpture, with two exceptions, reflected a similar emphasis on postwar work; but these were but part of a larger selection of sculpture that (with a few omissions) offers an international survey of contemporary sculpture.

The adventure of Cubism determined much of the future course of twentieth-century art. Cubist painting lasted longer than the short-lived Fauve movement, and its influence reached considerably further. The significance of Cubism may be compared with that of another important development, Abstract Expressionism, which took place four decades later in the United States.

Nelson Rockefeller owned several major works painted in France during Cubism's heroic years, between 1907 and 1917. Taken together, they illustrate the development of Cubism, while individually, they characterize the personal styles of the three dominant Cubist masters—Georges Braque, Pablo Picasso, and Juan Gris. A consort to these works is Umberto Boccioni's famous Futurist triptych, *States of Mind*, painted in Milan in 1911 and shown in Paris the next year.

Picasso's *Harvesters*, 1907, the earliest and least known of these pictures, followed soon after his *Demoiselles d'Avignon*. Quickly painted, it is intense and brilliantly colored. The *Harvesters* shows five haymakers at the left, a wain in the background, and at the right a tree and two cows. The scene recalls the landscape of the Andorra valley where Picasso had spent the previous summer. As articulated by color and form, the spatial relationships between the figures are unexpected, audacious, and perhaps unique in Picasso's art. Although the distortions and varying perspectives announce stylistic developments of the next ten years, the *Harvesters* cannot be considered as even a proto-Cubist painting; it is one of Picasso's few Fauve essays.

In Paris in the early months of 1908 and 1909, Picasso painted two versions of a seated woman with a mandolin, one nude, the other dressed. During winter 1910, he twice repeated the same theme: in *Girl with a Mandolin (Fanny Tellier)* and in an oval composition, *Woman with a Mandolin*.

The monochromatic *Girl with a Mandolin* is essential to a review of Cubism—indeed, to any exposition of twentieth-century art. It is an explicit summary of early Analytic Cubism. It is one of Picasso's clearest solutions to a formal problem: the human body as a subject for Cubist analysis. In *Girl with a Mandolin*, two rounded forms—the prominent right breast, and the body of the mandolin—reflect the plastic and sculptural concerns of Analytic Cubism. The musical instrument is modeled with greater realism than the human anatomy, whose forms are for the most

Pablo Picasso. *Woman with a Mandolin*. 1910.
Oil on canvas. Oval, 31½ × 25½ inches
(80 × 64.8 cm).
Private collection.

Pablo Picasso. *Study for The Violin*. 1912.
Charcoal on paper. 24⅝ × 18⅝ inches
(62 × 47.3 cm).
Private collection.

Pablo Picasso. *Harvesters*. 1907.
Oil on canvas. 25 ½ × 32 inches (64.8 × 81.3 cm).
Bequeathed to The Museum of Modern Art, New York.

part flattened and squared. In addition to the breast and mandolin, two smaller areas, the eye and the cursive chignon, relieve the system of straight planes that reduces the figure to geometric shapes and displaces, blocks, and composes a generally ordered structure.

It is tempting to speculate how a Futurist painter might have viewed the same subject. Picasso's woman, however, is in repose. Her head inclines gently, and her playing is without movement. The background, against which the body seems suspended, is more obscure. A stretched accordion of solid rectangles, it is not immediately intelligible.

At this time, the friendship between Braque and Picasso was at its most intimate, and for a few months their personal styles were so similar as to seem interchangeable. Braque painted the same subject in the same pose at least twice; and many years later, Alfred Barr wrote Nelson Rockefeller that he had discovered a drawing by Braque that directly copies Picasso's *Girl with a Mandolin.*

Six still lifes in the Rockefeller collection illustrate the further evolution of Cubism. Two were small, compact paintings by Picasso. Approximately the same size, they

invite comparison. In the earlier, *Still Life: Le Torero,* painted at Céret in summer 1911, the bottle of rum, carafe, and glasses are transformed into a cascade of straight lines and planes. The objects themselves have all but disappeared, and there is no distinction between background and foreground—or, as Nelson Rockefeller said, the "subject matter drops into the background." The forms are completely fragmented. Their decomposition is starkly relieved by the placement of the black letters, "Le T . . ." and "Tau[reau]." But the painting has nothing to do with bulls or bullfighters. The painted imitation of printed letters is a formal, not contextual, element of the composition, and a prelude to collage. The picture, which, with the exception of the letters, shows Picasso at his most abstract and Cubism at its most extreme, was formerly owned by the artist's close friend, the French poet Paul Eluard.

In Picasso's later *Still Life: "Job,"* 1916, the monochromes of Analytic Cubism have been replaced by a brighter, wider range of colors. On a fringed tablecloth sit a bowl of grapes, a bottle of rum, and a pack of cigarettes, whose brand name lends the painting its title. Although the

Georges Braque. *Parc des Carrières, St. Denis*. 1909–10.
Oil on canvas. 16 × 17⅞ inches (40.6 × 45.4 cm).
Thyssen-Bornemisza Collection.

arrangement of the objects is completely free, their forms are more clearly defined, and thus more readable than in *Le Torero*. In contrast to the painted letters in that picture, the letters of "Job" identify an object, the pack of cigarettes. The textures of the painting's surface, also, are more varied; actual grains of sand and ash have been mixed with the paint. A pointillist technique, introduced into Cubism two years previously, further enlivens several passages.

"Job," which may be regarded as a collage made without paper or paste, could have been painted only after Picasso's experience of that medium. It anticipates a direction of Synthetic Cubism, which became increasingly decorative and, in Nelson Rockefeller's collection, culminated with Picasso's sumptuous *Pitcher and Bowl of Fruit,* 1931.

Although Cubism was considered a revolutionary style at the time it was developed, actually it evolved from a study of Paul Cézanne, and put to new uses many of his concepts. The introduction of collage was far more radical, for here disparate objects and materials, usually of paper, were affixed to the picture's surface. Since these elements were used to describe things rather than people or land-

scapes, Cubist collages are almost always still lifes. Three examples in the Rockefeller collection are alike in their iconography: the references to music so favored by Braque, Picasso, and Gris. Although these works demonstrate the personal techniques of the respective artists as makers of collage, more important is the fact that they share a common aesthetic. In these constructions trompe l'oeil—in the past a virtuoso variation of still-life painting—is achieved by the use of actual materials rather than by illusionistic imitation.

Picasso's *Guitar*, 1913, a painterly collage, is completely constructed of a variety of papers, including, somewhat exceptionally, a clipping from a Spanish newspaper. Braque's *Clarinet*, also 1913, appears less cluttered and more classic. It is, without a doubt, the most elegant of all his collages. Although elements of Braque's *Clarinet* are bound to canvas, essentially it is a drawing in black, brown, and charcoal, with large areas of white untouched. The paraphernalia of the still life are arranged within an oval, a shape particularly favored by the Cubists. Sometimes the canvas is mounted on an oval stretcher; sometimes, as here, the oval floats within a rectangle. The *Clarinet*, with its order, balance, and symmetry, was one of Nelson Rockefeller's favorite pictures.

Gris was the most representational, and perhaps the most lucid, of the Cubist painters. In the summer of 1914, when he was twenty-seven, Gris fled wartime Paris. For personal reasons, he could not return to Spain, and he settled instead near the border at Collioure, a small fishing village on the Mediterranean. When he returned to Paris in November, he brought with him six paintings and three collages—one of which was the *Guitar, Bottle, and Glass* in the Rockefeller collection. Like Braque's *Clarinet*, Gris's *Guitar, Bottle, and Glass* is an oval still life contained within a rectangle, this time a vertical one. Its intermingled combinations of pasted papers, paint, and drawing are exquisitely resolved and are very characteristic of Gris. The checkered pattern is also typical of his art. The contrasts of gray and black, green and brown, are warm and subdued. The multiple views of the glass illustrate perfectly the Cubists' preoccupation with the presentation of several aspects of the same object at the same time. The guitar also serves as table, with a leg breaking through the oval.

Gris spent most of 1917 in Paris. Although by this time the Cubists had abandoned collage, his austere and soaring *Sideboard* owes much to its inventions. Cubism was never wholly abstract, and Gris himself best described his aims in a letter to his friend, the dealer Daniel-Henry Kahnweiler: "I would like to continue the tradition of painting with plastic means while bringing to it a new aesthetic based on the intellect. I think one can quite well take over Chardin's means without taking over either the appearance of his pictures or his conception of reality. . . . I hope that ultimately I shall be able to express very precisely, and by means of pure intellectual elements, an imaginary reality. This really amounts to a sort of painting which is inaccurate but precise, just the opposite of bad painting which is accurate but not precise."

Three other paintings in the Rockefeller collection also belong to these heroic years and are stylistically allied to Cubism; indeed, they derive from it. The content of these paintings by Boccioni, however, is quite different; it evokes "states of mind," and is a subjective illustration of modern man's preoccupation with his own emotions.

The Futurists, and Boccioni in particular, adapted the language of Cubism to different purposes. Unlike the Cubists, the Futurists considered themselves against tradition. They were concerned with two problems: one formal—the visual description of movement; the other social—man's identity within a new and mechanized world of his own making. Their large compositions, with figures placed against the architectural setting of the modern city, throb with the pulse of metropolitan life. Late in 1911, after returning from Paris, where he experienced his first direct contact with Cubism, Boccioni painted *States of Mind*. The formal and stylistic differences between each of the panels that compose Boccioni's triptych are not subtle. The three paintings are unified by flat and consistent rhythms, which move tumultuously, diagonally or vertically, across the surface of each canvas.

The triptych is a dramatic narrative. Its interrelated subjects involve transportation, a machine, and people—those who travel by train, their method of departure, and the others who remain behind. The smoking locomotive in *The Farewells* divides a swelling crowd. The arabic numerals stenciled on the cab derive, of course, from Cubism; but their use here is not completely formal, since, like the black roman numerals "I" and "III" painted at the right and left of the central panel, *Those Who Go*, to designate first- and third-class carriages, they serve to indicate parts of the train. In *Those Who Stay*, visitors retreat across the station's platform. Their movement is arrested, dragging, and sad, spaced within the vertical accents that grid the picture. In *Those Who Go*, the train's speed is rendered by diagonal and rounded thrusts, which oscillate and unite the staring faces of the passengers with the landscape that unfolds before them.

Braque's vertical *Table*, 1930, and Picasso's horizontal *Pitcher and Bowl of Fruit*, 1931, lie beyond Cubism's historic confines. Both are large paintings, decorative in conception. Their perspectives remain flattened, as in Cubism, but the overall patterns of these still lifes are less rigorous and more ornate. The Braque belongs to a series of paintings of this kind of round-topped table that continues into the 1930s. The table, bowl of fruit, mandolin, and sheets of music recall the iconography of Cubism, as do the staccato, pointillist brush strokes (which also occur in the Picasso). As in the Picasso, the forms are more flowing and the colors less inhibited than in earlier Cubist works. The textured grains that enrich the surface of the painting deliberately reduce the sheen of the oil paint.

There are fewer kinds of objects in Picasso's still life, but its composition is more intricate. Although the silhouettes of the forms are isolated and heavily outlined, their spatial relationships are never clarified. The brilliant colors shine through the heavy borders of the shapes with the luminosity of stained glass within its leading. Beneath the dark outlines, ribbons of lighter colors cross the surface of the painting in straight lines and sweeping curves.

Fernand Léger, who was influenced by Cubism earlier than Gris, stands somewhat apart from the two Spaniards or his fellow Frenchman, Braque. His paintings are direct and rarely speak with the lyric qualities that characterize Cubism. His forms are seldom transparent, as in Cubist painting; they are volumes, cylindrical and architectonic. Léger does not attempt to examine different aspects of an object; rather, he repeats its shape. His painting seems most germane to Cubism between 1910 and 1914; in 1912, he was also influenced by Futurism.

World War I disbanded the unity of the Cubist painters. Léger was drafted into the French Army in 1914, served in the engineering corps, and was wounded and discharged three years later. His observation of war machines helped him to develop a personal style that he had begun to conceive as early as 1910. The small, brilliantly colored *Armistice*, 1918, with its almost enameled surface, parades a profusion of flags (one American) seen from a window. This is not a glorification of the modern metropolis; the little painting is intimate and, for Léger, unexpectedly lively.

Like so many works in Nelson Rockefeller's collection, a second painting by Léger, *Woman with a Book*, 1923, seems difficult rather than pretty. To Léger, who was strongly influenced by the machine aesthetics of Le Corbusier and Amédée Ozenfant, there is no distinction between man, animal, and object: "One may consider the human figure not for its sentimental value but only for its plastic value. That is why in the evolution of my work since 1905 until now the human figure has remained purposely inexpressive.'' The woman stands like a hieratic statue, confronting the modern world. This statue can neither move nor breathe; its frontality is aggressive and unrelieved. The neck rises like a column, the arms are rigged to the body, the hair is burnished metal. The figure is sexless, the face plain, symmetric, immobile, and devoid of all expression. The beautiful pattern of the composition owes as much to the impedimenta of book and flowers as it does to the woman herself.

Léger's preoccupation with mechanical forms was expressed two-dimensionally. The sculptor Raymond Duchamp-Villon, however, composed forms in three dimensions, which interact as do the elements of a collage, to produce a construction.

In World War I, Duchamp-Villon enlisted with the Cuirassiers and, like Léger, saw the terrible new machines made by man. Duchamp-Villon was confounded by the anachronism of the horse as a means of transportation. He became so obsessed with this paradox that, in 1914, he decided actually to transform the horse into a machine—a noble one. He sought to reduce, reveal, and combine in sculpture the anatomy, spirit, and movement of the animal. Working in plaster, he made seven small statues, and as the series progressed, the figure of the horse became increasingly abstract. After his death in 1918, the last of these versions was enlarged twice—first, in 1930–31, to forty inches high, and later, in 1966, to almost five feet high. The most dramatic, larger version, often known as *Le Cheval majeur*, was part of the Rockefeller collection. This beast is itself a hero, an equestrian monument without a rider.

Fernand Léger. *Armistice*. 1918.
Oil on canvas. 21¾ × 15 inches (55.3 × 38.1 cm).
Private collection.

Fernand Léger. *Gears*. 1935–37?
Pencil and wash on paper. 7⅜ × 5⅜ inches (18.8 × 13.7 cm).

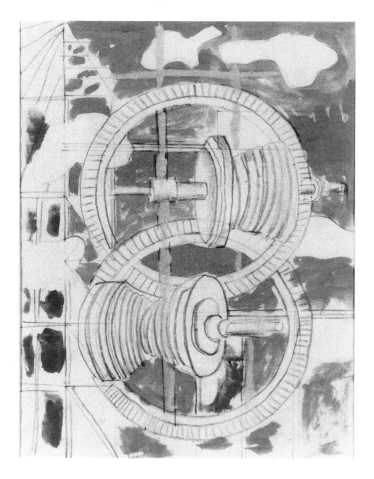

To appreciate and understand the simultaneous and different aspects of *The Horse*, the spectator should walk around the sculpture, or the piece itself should turn. Its dynamic spiral recalls Boccioni's sculptured still life, *Development of a Bottle in Space*, and indeed Duchamp-Villon frequently seems closer to Futurism than to Cubism. Both Duchamp-Villon and Constantin Brancusi had wished to see final versions of certain of their works in stainless steel, but unfortunately the posthumous casts of Duchamp-Villon's horse were all done in bronze.

Brancusi's *Bird in Space* exists in several versions. The bronze in the Rockefeller collection measures more than six feet high and is one of the tallest in the series that Brancusi began in 1923. The balanced taper of the solid rounded form soars with simple grace and strength. Brancusi's elegant monolith contrasts with the open, somehow

33

more vulnerable, interacting parts of Duchamp-Villon's horse.

Brancusi was not a Cubist, and his aesthetic is quite different in its purpose, origins, and development from that of Duchamp-Villon. He sought the embodiment of spirit, not character; the visualization of motion, not movement. Brancusi distills meaning; he was never concerned with the specific. Unlike the Cubists, he did not analyze form into its component parts. Instead, he refined his subjects—for example, the bird—into universal generalizations.

Two other sculptors, Jacques Lipchitz and Alexander Archipenko, who were working in Paris at about the same time, did translate the canons of Cubism into three dimensions. Among the Cubists, Gris was closest to Lipchitz, whose *Seated Man with Guitar*, 1922, carved from basalt, is one of the most successful in a series of Cubist interpretations of guitar players begun in 1914. It was subsequently cast in bronze in an edition of seven. The major work by Lipchitz in the Rockefeller collection is one of the artist's greatest monuments, *Song of the Vowels*, 1931–32.

An exhibition of Cubist sculpture limited to the two decades after 1909 might demonstrate the significance of Archipenko. It would be revealing, and his stature would increase, if his work could be viewed in context with earlier works by Picasso, Duchamp-Villon, and Lipchitz, and contrasted with sculpture by Henri Laurens and Ossip Zadkine. Like the Lipchitz *Seated Man with Guitar*, Archipenko's *Standing Woman*, 1923, is directly carved and is small in size. It repeats one of his earlier plaster figures and coincides in time with the first wood carvings by Henry Moore. The medium, mahogany, is unusual in Archipenko's work.

The ramifications of Cubism and the influence of collage were not limited to France. In The Netherlands, Piet Mondrian and his friends developed a geometric and rectangular style, derived from Cubism; but unlike Cubism, it resulted in complete abstraction. Mondrian's *Large Composition A*, 1920, almost exactly square, pushes the liberties of Cubism to an extreme and completely disengages the artist from any reference to the object.

In France, the Cubists ceased to make collages after 1917. In Germany, however, several of the Dadaists adopted collage and, indeed, transformed it, often with wit. Kurt Schwitters, whose approach to the medium was highly individual, continued to compose collages throughout his career. His constructions are abstract and vary considerably in size; they rarely conceal the shapes and origins of the pasted papers that he collected from the debris of daily life to use in them. Nelson Rockefeller owned a bouquet of small collages by Schwitters ranging in date from 1921 to 1946.

The flowing freedom of Art Nouveau, the first truly international modern style, was a major source for the conflagration of Expressionism, which spread through Europe shortly after 1900. If one accepts a broad definition, Expressionism is a form of Mannerism. The visual articulation of emotion and the inner self, and the subjective interpretation of observed form, need not necessarily be keyed to trauma. The employment of autonomous color and stylistic distortion can be decorative, as well as dramatic. When the use of these devices is pushed to an extreme, however, the result may seem pathological.

Within the span of a relatively few years, Expressionist styles developed almost simultaneously in France with the Fauves, in Germany with the group known as Die Brücke, and with two Russian contemporaries, Alexey Jawlensky and Wassily Kandinsky. Though their styles evolved independently, there were personal contacts among many of these artists and numerous crosscurrents of influence.

In contrast to the brotherhood of Die Brücke, founded in Dresden in 1905, the Fauves were never a cohesive group. Neither were they obsessed by modern man's discovery of his own psyche, the exploration of which so insistently haunted the Expressionists in Germany. Fauve painting is structured on form rather than on content; its patterns are bold and bright. The Fauve painters were particularly attracted to views of rivers and ports, always with reference to the safe, adjacent land. In 1905, Henri Matisse and his family began to summer in Collioure, the small fishing village near the Spanish border in which Gris was to spend summer 1914. It was at Collioure that Matisse and André Derain painted the first Fauve pictures. Matisse's landscape of the harbor of Collioure in the Rockefeller collection is, however, somewhat later.

In *View of Collioure and the Sea*, 1911, Matisse observes the scene almost as if it were a stage set viewed from the balcony of a theater. Looking down and through a proscenium of trees painted dark blue, one sees the small peninsula, which protects the waters of the bay. The overall design of the painting is not characteristically Fauve, for the contrast between the silhouette of the foreground and the landscape below is calculated and disciplined. The colors and shapes, however, are painted with the utmost freedom.

Matisse was in his mid-thirties before his art found its direction. He was the dominant personality of the Fauves, whose loose association was of short duration. Like most of his companions, he abandoned the wild freedom of the Fauve palette for more controlled but generally joyous color.

The Fauves first exhibited publicly in Paris in autumn 1905. Shortly thereafter an American family, the Steins, consisting of Gertrude, her brothers Leo and Michael, and Michael's wife Sarah, became Matisse's first important patrons. (They were also important early patrons of Picasso; his sheet of drawings, *Study for "The Actor" with Profiles of Fernande*, 1904–05, owned by Nelson Rockefeller, was formerly in the collection of Gertrude Stein.) Other American collectors also became interested in Matisse's art—Dr. Claribel and Miss Etta Cone of Baltimore among them. Only one other American family was to have as long an involvement with Matisse: the Rockefellers. The relationship, which began in 1930, lasted nearly twenty-five years, until the artist's death.

The *Reclining Nude*, 1907, in Nelson Rockefeller's collection, is a translation into bronze of one of Matisse's major Fauve paintings, the *Blue Nude* of the same year. The statue of the *Reclining Nude* was in turn incorporated by Matisse into later paintings, and subsequently, in 1929, its subject and pose were again repeated in one of his sculptures. It is also related to drawings and prints by Matisse. Similarly, a second Matisse bronze owned by Nelson Rockefeller, the *Seated Nude*, 1925, relates intimately to another smaller bronze by Matisse as well as to a series of lithographs of odalisques, such as the rare *Odalisque in Striped Pantaloons*, 1925.

Henri Matisse. *Odalisque*. 1929.
Oil on canvas. 18¼ × 21⅞ inches (46.3 × 55.3 cm).
The Museum of Modern Art, New York. Nelson A. Rockefeller Bequest.

Another important early patron of Matisse was a Russian businessman, Sergei I. Shchukin, who in the decade preceding World War I was the greatest collector of modern French painting in the world. Early in 1909, he commissioned from Matisse two murals, *Dance* and *Music*, for the stair landing of his house in Moscow. Final versions of these were completed by Matisse in 1910 and are now in The Hermitage in Leningrad. The first version of the *Dance*, painted early in 1909, lay for years rolled up in Matisse's studio before being sold in 1936 to Walter P. Chrysler, Jr. In 1963, it was bought by Nelson Rockefeller, who generously presented this great and historic masterpiece of the modern movement to The Museum of Modern Art in honor of Alfred Barr, his friend for over three decades.

Another of Matisse's earlier paintings owned by Nelson Rockefeller is the *Italian Woman*, 1915, which had previously belonged to the great New York collector of modern art, John Quinn. Like Picasso's *Girl with a Mandolin (Fanny Tellier)*, the *Italian Woman* is one of several masterpieces in a gallery of modern portraits. The painting, with its warm colors and bold ellipse, owes much to Matisse's observation of Cubism. It is one of a series of monumental single figures that he painted between 1913 and 1917.

In his paintings of the nude and his use of the female figure as decoration, Amedeo Modigliani is closer to Matisse than any other artist painting in Paris in the years around World War I. His career was brief; he died at the age of thirty-six. He studied sculpture with Brancusi for a short time and executed a few works in that medium, but he is best known as a painter. His range of subjects is much more limited than Matisse's; with the exception of three landscapes, Modigliani's paintings are confined to likenesses of his friends, acquaintances, and casual pickups. His nudes glorify the female form, which he adored. Like Matisse, he always worked from the model. The Rockefeller collection brought together in fascinating association the two bronze nudes by Matisse and Modigliani's *The Dreamer*, 1918, which is similar to them in pose.

Modigliani's reclining nudes offer the only horizontal images in his art. Silhouetted against a dark background

Gabrielle Münter. *Boating (Kahnfahrt)*. 1910.
Oil on canvas. 22 × 19¾ inches (55.9 × 50.2 cm).

almost immediately behind her, the elongated torso of *The Dreamer* stretches diagonally across the picture plane. The contours of her body and the features of her face are soft, and more sculpturally rounded than in Modigliani's other likenesses of women. The model's expression is somewhat wistful, her pose pliant and supine. Modigliani brings felicitously to a close a Mannerist tradition of Italianate painting in France that goes back to the School of Fontainebleau in the sixteenth century.

The passionate tragedy of his life has cast Modigliani, like Vincent van Gogh, as a romantic hero. His actual achievement lies somewhat outside the mainstream of twentieth-century art; but, in his series of some twenty nudes, what glorious paintings he made!

Two Russian contemporaries of the Fauves, Jawlensky and Kandinsky, evolved a style similar to theirs. Their early paintings, however, seem flatter than those of the Fauves and seldom attempt illusionistic perspective. Although their colors appear even more vivid, perhaps because of the contrasting use of black, they are, in fact, more naturalistic. The opaque tonality of these colors, as well as the method of application, owes some inspiration to the folk arts of Russia and Bavaria.

It is difficult to believe that Jawlensky painted the haunting *Cottage in the Woods* as early as 1903, although it is so marked on its reverse. The placement of the tree and its shadow is daring, and the panel bristles with divisionist color.

In 1907, Jawlensky met Matisse in Paris, and in the same year renewed his acquaintance with Kandinsky in Munich. For a short while, the friendship of the two Russians became as close and intense as that of Braque and Picasso in Paris a few years later. In 1908 and 1909, they summered with Marianne von Werefkin and Gabrielle Münter in Murnau, a village in southern Bavaria. It was there that Kandinsky painted *Autumn Landscape, Murnau*, 1908.

The forms in this painting, like those in Jawlensky's *Spanish Girl*, 1912, are heavily outlined in black. The decorative use of discordant color, however, allies the two Russians with the Fauves rather than with the German Expressionists. In the Jawlensky, the model's head characteristically fills the rectangle of the picture. The vulgarity of her coarse, heavily made-up features is relieved by the headdress, whose haloed contour softens the flat angularity of her face. *The Spanish Girl* is painted in oil on paper, a medium favored for several years by Jawlensky and Kandinsky. Its use may explain why some of their pictures of this period so often lack transparency and depth of color.

Kees van Dongen, the one member of the Fauves who was not French by birth, was the stylistic link between the Fauves and The Bridge brotherhood in Dresden. In 1908, they invited van Dongen to become a member of their group, and he exhibited a number of prints and drawings with them in Germany. His *Woman in a Large Hat* was also painted in that year. Its technique remains Fauve, but its style is as mundane as the subject is elegant, foreshadowing the later direction of his art.

Georges Rouault was for a time associated with the Fauves and continued to a later date the tradition of Expressionist painting in France. *The Judge*, painted by Rouault in 1930, was a gift to Nelson Rockefeller from his mother. It is impossible not to wonder whether Nelson Rockefeller did not subconsciously recall *The Judge* when, in 1949, he purchased Max Beckmann's *Woman with a Parrot*, 1946. The paintings have in common a suggestion of allegory, the profile view, the contours of the shoulders and arms, the heavy outlines, and even a rectangle in the background.

Beckmann was not directly allied with German Expressionism, but his *Woman with a Parrot*, a relatively late work, is the only painting in the Rockefeller collection that was in any way related to that tradition. It was painted in Amsterdam in 1946, a year after the liberation of The Netherlands (where Beckmann had settled after the Nazis, in 1936, declared his art "degenerate"), and a year before he and his wife emigrated to the United States. The picture of a woman seated beside a piano is as mannered as Modigliani's *Dreamer*, and as handsome.

Although Nelson Rockefeller owned no works by the German Expressionists active in the first quarter of the twentieth-century, he did own a number of works in sculpture by their contemporaries: Ernst Barlach, Georg Kolbe, Gerhard Marcks, and Wilhelm Lehmbruck. Of his two cast-stone pieces by Lehmbruck, the small *Dancer*, 1913–14, was purchased in 1939. The elegant *Torso*, 1910, he received in 1950 as a gift from his friend Wallace K. Harrison, the architect of Rockefeller Center.

Certainly the greatest Expressionist painter of the twentieth-century is Picasso. His most Expressionist work in the collection is a painting of the mid-1930s. During

1934, he had painted several vertical compositions of two girls seated at a table, their eyes downcast as they read, write, or draw. In February 1935, he resumed the theme in two large horizontal paintings, which are quite similar in composition: each has a mirror at the left, a table with a bouquet of flowers, and two girls seated on the floor—one asleep, the other drawing.

Of the two paintings, Nelson Rockefeller's was the larger. To a Picasso enthusiast the *Interior with a Girl Drawing* is particularly fascinating. The sinuous and heavily outlined curves evident in the related paintings of the previous year are here modified by angular accents, particularly in the furniture and the figure at the right. Underneath the picture lies another one, which Picasso had photographed and elaborately annotated in a drawing before painting over it. This first version was even more angular, and it differs in several other respects: the table was smaller, the background uncurtained, the two women farther apart,

Ernst Barlach. *The Skeptic.* 1937.
Bronze. 19¾ × 10⅝ × 7⅜ inches
(50.2 × 27 × 18.8 cm).

and the one at the right lacking the garland of flowers which, in the final version, crowns her head.

In 1930, Picasso was awarded First Prize at the 29th Carnegie International Exhibition in Pittsburgh. One member of the three-man jury was Matisse, who, before returning to France, visited the two most important Matisse collections in the United States, those of the Barnes Foundation in Merion, Pennsylvania, and of Miss Etta Cone in Baltimore, and then came to New York, where Mrs. Rockefeller, eager to meet him, gave a dinner in his honor. Nelson Rockefeller was at the time in the Dutch East Indies. Less than a year later, Mrs. Rockefeller purchased for herself a small oil by Matisse, *Odalisque*, which she presented to her son in 1932 when he became a trustee of The Museum of Modern Art; it was his first significant acquisition of a modern painting.

In that year, the great complex of Rockefeller Center was under construction in New York. Nelson Rockefeller and his mother hoped that Matisse might be persuaded to paint one of the three murals for the large entrance hall of 30 Rockefeller Plaza. Matisse refused. In 1938, however, Nelson Rockefeller was more successful. He was able to commission a very much smaller, more intimate mural—the overmantel that surrounds a fireplace in his New York apartment. Brightly painted and decorative, it is a gracious and luxurious ornament.

In 1954, Nelson Rockefeller sought Matisse again. His mother had died in 1948, and he asked Matisse to design the stained glass for a memorial rose window in the east wall of the Union Church of Pocantico Hills—the church with which she and her family had been closely associated. Matisse, who remembered Mrs. Rockefeller with affection and respect, accepted the commission.

Nelson Rockefeller's reaction to any work of art, like his reaction to people, was immediate, direct, and always interested. He was primarily concerned with the formal elements of an object: its shape, its color, the resolution of its composition. Because he was not particularly attracted by subject matter, there were few paintings in his collection that were descriptive or that invited literary associations. This may explain why he chose relatively few Surrealist pictures.

Two of his acquisitions, however, are major works that anticipate the painted dreams and illogical juxtapositions of the Surrealists. The earlier of these is *The Dream* by the "Douanier" Rousseau. Painted in 1910, shortly before the artist's death, it was his last great effort and the consummation of his entire career. Though scorned by the academic critics and laughed at by the public, the paintings of the self-taught Henri Rousseau had qualities that attracted the attention and acclaim of artists as diverse as Edgar Degas and Henri de Toulouse-Lautrec, the Cubists Braque and Picasso, and later the Surrealists.

First shown in the United States in 1933, *The Dream* was acquired in that year by Sidney Janis for his private collection. Twenty years later he told Alfred Barr that he intended to part with it, and would give the Musem the first chance to acquire it. Mr. Barr immediately brought this to the attention of Nelson Rockefeller, who knew the masterpiece well and deliberated for some time whether to purchase it for his own collection or for the Museum. However, when he discovered that the painting was too large for the wall of his living room in the capital, he generously gave it to the Museum on the occasion of its Twenty-fifth Anniversary in 1954.

In 1949, Nelson Rockefeller acquired for his own collection another masterpiece, one of the forerunners of Surrealism. This was Giorgio de Chirico's *The Song of Love*. It was painted in Paris in 1914, when the artist was becoming particularly interested in still life, after having previously created a series of pictures showing silent city squares, peopled only by statues set amid the architecture. In his still lifes, inanimate objects become larger in scale and importance. They are combined in enigmatic juxtapositions whose effect is all the more disquieting because of the realistic manner in which they are painted.

Until shortly before its acquisition by Nelson Rockefeller, *The Song of Love* remained in Paris, where it was widely influential among French and Belgian artists. In 1924, ten years after this picture was painted, the French poet André Breton founded Surrealism—a movement in literature as well as in the visual arts. Surrealism pursued two courses in exploring the subconscious mind. One, following the lead of de Chirico, was illusionistic. An artist in the Rockefeller collection who continued this tradition was Paul Delvaux, in his late painting, *The Watchman, II*, 1961. The parallel course—free, automatic, and biomorphic—is far more in evidence in the Rockefeller collection.

Jean Arp's lively *Man with a Moustache*, c. 1924, is one of a series of compositions, rendered in oil on cardboard with cutouts, which bear no relation whatsoever to illusionism or reality. Arp, who remained the most abstract of the Surrealists, reached his full stature with sculpture in the round. His works, although nonrepresentational, nevertheless express the principles of growth and transformation that one finds in nature. By the mid-1930s, Arp had already mastered this style, as for example in *Shell Crystal*, 1938, and several superb examples of his later work in stone, concrete, and bronze.

The Catalan artist Joan Miró was a friend and neighbor of Arp in Montmartre in 1925–26 and was certainly influenced to some extent by the latter's biomorphic inventions. But, like his compatriot Picasso, Miró never thought of himself as an abstractionist. Two of his paintings in the Rockefeller collection were extraordinary. Both are large in size; one was conceived as a mural, the other as a cartoon for a tapestry. The earlier belongs to a series painted in Barcelona in 1933, to which Miró refused to give titles. The method of conception was unusual in Miró's art. Before he began to paint, he made preliminary sketches in collage. Such studies, in his own words, "served me as points of departure for paintings. I did not copy the collages. I merely let them suggest shapes to me...." This particularly disciplined work was a self-imposed experiment, a temporary effort to control the automatic spontaneity of his brush. The austere and anchored forms of the final paintings are somber in color.

Hirondelle/Amour, 1934, a much more joyous song of love than de Chirico's, offers a vivid contrast to Miró's untitled painting of the previous year. Its movements and colors are free; figures, faces, limbs swirl swiftly through the sky, in which Miró also set a star and sun. Although it is difficult for the eye to rest on any single detail, the arrangement of forms is not restless, but graceful and continuously flowing, like the flight of the swallow suggested by the title. The evocative title itself is typically Surrealist; here, the calligraphy of its letters is incorporated into the composition.

Some of Miró's paintings of the late 1920s have a certain kinship with the art of Paul Klee, to which Miró had been introduced by some of his Surrealist colleagues. Although the exquisite clarity of Klee's vision remains independent from that of any of his contemporaries, his inventive fantasy has many affinities with Surrealism. James Thrall Soby described his work as "the chamber music of modern art." Among the Klees in the Rockefeller collection were two vivid characterizations of imaginary people, *Sharp Profile*, 1924, and *The Jester*, 1927; and two later paintings, *Fear*, 1934, and *Heroic Strokes of the Bow*, 1938, which are less literal, and transcend mere description of persons or objects.

His *Sharp Profile*, depicting a haughty matron, shares the humorous approach of Arp's witty *Man with a Moustache* of the same year. The technique of Klee's drawing is particularly inventive and is peculiar to his watercolors of the early 1920s. The black lines are "transferred" by placing a sheet of paper over an inked surface and drawing on it with a hard pencil; the pressure of the pencil causes ink to adhere to the verso of the sheet, registering the drawn image in reverse.

The Jester, one of Klee's merriest performers, also presents a "sharp profile." Klee drew and painted several other versions of this figure. Here, the comedian is a juggler; the sharp-edged shapes of the gnomelike tatterdemalion's eye, hand, and costume are set in motion by the circle of five spinning balls.

Fear is painted on burlap. Its pale, hallucinatory image exemplifies several of Klee's theories of form, movement, and line. At the right, fingers of unknown hands reach for the large rounded face, which stares at the unseen assailant with one anxiously fixed eye. This translation into visual terms of a state of mind was painted in the same year that the Nazis seized and burned an edition of a book of Klee's drawings. The artist had already sought refuge in Switzerland a few months before.

Heroic Strokes of the Bow is painted in blue and black. It distills the essence of a specific shape, its motion, and even its sound: the lines simultaneously represent the act of bowing as well as the bow itself. The special music that Klee, the violinist, heard he made visible in the joined lines, curved and straight, that form musical staves. Within this continuous contour, he placed rhythmic beats, notes, and rests. The music is a swelling crescendo. At its close, toward the bottom of the painting, Klee marked the suggestion of a bass clef and a final release.

Alberto Giacometti, whose first sculptural works were strongly influenced by the Cubists, came into contact with the Surrealists in 1928 and for the next few years participated in their publications and exhibitions. For a long period of time, he continued to alternate between works that explored the unconscious and those more closely related to the visual world and its expression in plastic terms. Three bronzes, made within a ten-year span and all depicting women, reveal various aspects of his art. The pregnant figure, *Spoon Woman*, 1926, is a concave monolith, which in spite of its abstraction is still highly erotic. Its compact

Paul Klee. *The Jester.* 1927.
Oil on cardboard. 28½ × 18¾ inches
(72.4 × 47.6 cm).
Private collection.

curves contrast with the angular, savagely scattered forms of the *Woman with Her Throat Cut,* 1932. This, in turn, is entirely different from the headless *Nude,* 1932–36, a serene, immobile statue that deliberately recalls an archaic style; its attenuation already foreshadows the elongated proportions of Giacometti's later figures, such as those in *City Square,* 1948.

During World War II, many artists left Europe for the United States, some as temporary refugees and others to remain. Several of them were Surrealists—Max Ernst, André Masson, Yves Tanguy, Salvador Dali, and Matta among them. Their influence was especially important for the birth of the style that developed in New York during the 1940s and came to be known as Abstract Expressionism or "the new American painting." A focus for the showing of many of these European artists and for the young Americans whose own styles were just beginning to emerge was Peggy Guggenheim's gallery, Art of This Century, which opened in 1942 and was designed by Frederick J. Kiesler. This Vienna-born architect, designer, and sculptor, who had come to the United States as a theater designer in 1926, had been associated with a succession of avant-garde movements since the early 1920s, and remained a pioneer until

his death in 1965, at age seventy-five. Among the most successful of his ambitious projects, articulated through the language of Surrealism, is the large and stunning *Galaxy.* Kiesler, who had made an earlier version of this construction, completed the final work in 1951. This unforgettable structure was described in 1952 as "a spatial sculpture . . . made of wood fashioned only with a saw and joined with wooden pegs. It measures twelve feet high, and the length of its longest crossbar is over fourteen feet. Kiesler . . . looks on *Galaxy* as a practical sculpture, to live with and within—to put in a garden, in a wooded grove or on a beach." In the same periodical Alfred Barr did more than describe the construction; he composed a poem. Within the posts of the wooden frame, Mr. Barr visualized four sailors, one flown, one swallowed, one shipwrecked, and the last damned:

> *Galaxy* is architecture for sky-gazers; its plan is a cross with arms raised in amazement; its major axis slopes abruptly toward a vanishing point like Borromini's false perspective in the Palazzo Spada; its four caryatids are a dolphin's spine, a hippocampus, a lobster claw and an ichthyosaur caressed by a boomerang; its lintels are driftwood and a comb-finned gar.
> *Galaxy* is a four-poster in which Sinbad, Jonah, Crusoe and Ahab may sit eternally, back to back, telling each other their stories, slowly, with low voices and credulous ears.
> *Galaxy* is a pergola built of jetsam where refugees from the compass and ruler may dry their nets in peace.
> *Galaxy* is a drifting raft where common sense, watched by the skeletons of the four winds, will die of thirst.
> *Galaxy* is a conspiracy for discrediting Cadillacs.
> *Galaxy* is the tomb of know-how, the supreme anti-technological gazebo.

Among the artists who left France during the war was Wifredo Lam, who returned to his native Cuba in 1941. After his early studies in Havana, Lam had lived first in Spain and then in Paris. There he met Picasso, who aided and deeply influenced him; and there, also, he joined the Surrealist group. As in many of Lam's works, *Chemical Nuptials,* 1944, retains the exotic atmosphere of the semi-tropics; it is a heraldic allegory that disquietingly marries birds and flowers.

Lam's painting is one of a number of works by Latin American artists in Nelson Rockefeller's collection. During the 1930s, he and his mother had become familiar with the work of the great Mexican muralists and had been responsible for commissioning murals from two of them, Diego Rivera and José Clemente Orozco.

Nelson Rockefeller's interest in the arts of the Latin American republics continued, and his collection included several examples in various mediums: *St. John's Day,* 1938, by the Mexican painter Julio Castellanos; the sculpture *Magical Apparatus, II,* 1954, by Edgar Negret of Colombia; a work of 1964 in tempera and knotted cloth on canvas by the Peruvian Jorge Eielson, called *Red Quipu;* and pieces by Emilio Rodriguez-Larrain y Balta, also from Peru, Rogelio Polesello of Argentina, and the Uruguayan Antonio Frasconi.

The Rockefeller collection's American paintings from the post–World War II period reveal a personal preference for Abstract Expressionism; indeed, during the 1950s Nelson Rockefeller was one of the foremost collectors of the movement. He acquired paintings by William Baziotes, James Brooks, Helen Frankenthaler, Adolph Gottlieb, Philip Guston, Grace Hartigan, Willem de Kooning, Morris Louis, Robert Motherwell, Mark Rothko, and Mark Tobey in the very years in which they were painted or first exhibited.

In 1950 and 1952, Mr. Rockefeller bought paintings by Jackson Pollock. He gave *Number 16, 1950* to the Museu de Arte Moderna in Rio de Janeiro; another, *Number 12, 1952*, was one of Pollock's masterpieces. That painting and three others of prime importance in the development of Abstract Expressionism: Arshile Gorky's *The Calendars*, 1946–47; Franz Kline's *Corinthian*, 1957; and Bradley Walk-

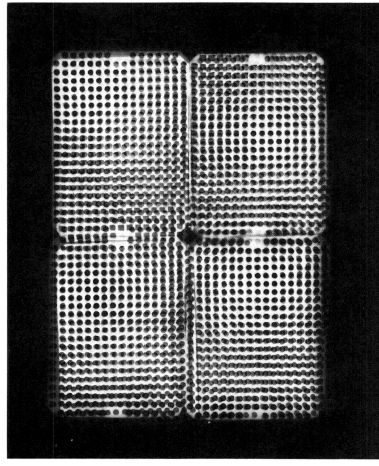

Rogelio Polesello. *Black*. 1966.
Synthetic polymer paint on canvas. 41¼ × 33⅜ inches (104.8 × 84.8 cm).
NHT.

Diego Rivera. *The Fruit Vendor*. 1921.
Oil on paper. 25 × 19 inches (63.5 × 48.3 cm).
Private collection.

Emilio Rodriguez-Larrain y Balta. *Mantilla and Carnations, XIII*. 1961.
Mixed mediums on paper, mounted on wood.
39 × 39 inches (99.1 × 99.1 cm).

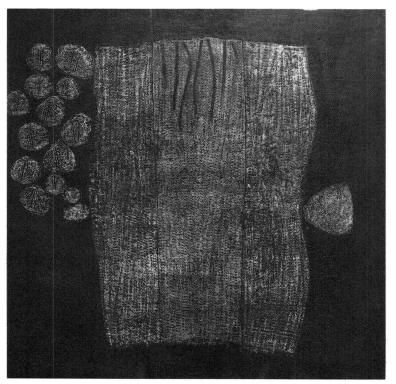

er Tomlin's *Number 18*, 1950, no longer exist. On the night of March 6, 1961, when Nelson Rockefeller had been governor of the state of New York for two years, fire swept the Executive Mansion in Albany. Fortunately, lives were spared; but some of his favorite paintings and prints were completely destroyed or badly damaged. The loss among his American paintings was particularly severe, for the four highly important pictures just named, as well as others, were among those burnt.

From the point of view of its significance for the development of Abstract Expressionism, perhaps the most serious of these losses was Gorky's *The Calendars*. Gorky was born in Armenia, and came to the United States when he was sixteen. Though his early style was modeled upon a succession of painters as disparate as Ingres, Cézanne, and Picasso, among others, he may be regarded as an authentic disciple of Surrealism. During the war years Gorky was close to the Surrealists who found refuge in the United States, including Breton himself, as well as the artists Ernst, Tanguy, Masson, and Matta.

In 1942, Gorky's art reached maturity. As the combined influences of Picasso, Miró, and Matta were absorbed, and as his style became increasingly defined in technique and imagery, his own vision was finally released. The large pictures done in 1946 and 1947, a year or so before his death, achieve a kind of heroic nobility. Among the most important of them was the five-foot-wide, opaquely colored *Calendars*, which Nelson Rockefeller acquired in 1950.

Gorky was a meticulous craftsman and usually made detailed studies on paper for his paintings. Although no specific drawing for *The Calendars* is known, a smaller, preliminary oil painting exists. *The Calendars* transforms an interior—a living room or studio—into an abstraction. The defined areas of space within the composition can be easily described: in the center foreground, a diagonal thrust; in the background, vertical planes of different colors. A table in the foreground displays a still life; above it, near the upper right corner of the painting, is a lampshade. An easel set with a picture appears at the left. In another room, at the right, a figure sits at some sort of drawing table. In the center of the canvas, an ovoid shape contains forms that may suggest burning logs.

The loss of *The Calendars* was all the more regrettable, because in 1946 about twenty-seven of Gorky's paintings in his studio in Connecticut had also been destroyed by fire. In June 1948, he committed suicide—the victim of illness, personal misfortunes, and what he regarded as a lack of adequate recognition of his contribution as an artist. In fact, full appreciation of Gorky's originality and his influence on the formation of the "new American painting" did not come until after his death.

As tragic as the loss of *The Calendars* was the damage to Pollock's *Number 12, 1952*, for the artist, like Gorky, was no longer living, and the painting was unique in his work. Early in 1952, Pollock had become dissatisfied with the series of large paintings in black enamel on white, unsized canvas, on which he had been engaged for some time. In revolt against the self-imposed discipline of black and white, he completely repainted two of these pictures by covering their surfaces with color. Understandably, the impasto of both paintings, *Blue Poles* and *Convergence*, is

Max Ernst. *Preistorico*. 1966.
Green glass (unique cast). 16⅝ × 8⅞ × 2⅝
inches (42.2 × 22.3 × 6.7 cm).
NHT.

thick; but Pollock's next large composition, *Number 12, 1952*, was much more thinly painted on a clean canvas, expressing his resolve to return to color. The easy continuity of its lines displayed the relaxed control of his previous black-and-white pictures, but this was the only large canvas in which Pollock composed broad areas of thinly washed colors. Skeins of liquid black played against great pools of almost pretty colors, whose transparency was heightened by glimpses of the dulled silver of aluminum paint. The contrast between the black lines and the limpid veils of color implied a limitless space; like many of Pollock's late works, *Number 12, 1952* was universal in concept, and was stated with dynamic intensity. Almost oriental in mood, this work on canvas, like Chinese or Japanese paintings on paper, was a masterful consummation of draftsmanship for painterly effect.

Tomlin, too, was dead when the fire in the Executive Mansion destroyed his painting *Number 18*, 1950. Fortunately Nelson Rockefeller was able to secure an earlier and not too dissimilar work by him, *Number 5*, 1949. Of the four major Abstract Expressionists whose work was lost, only Kline was still alive. He was naturally extremely distressed by the destruction of a picture that he considered one of his best; after some hesitation, he painted a second

Bradley Walker Tomlin. *Number 18*. 1950.
Oil on canvas. 78½ × 49 inches (199.4 × 124.5 cm).
Destroyed by fire, 1961.

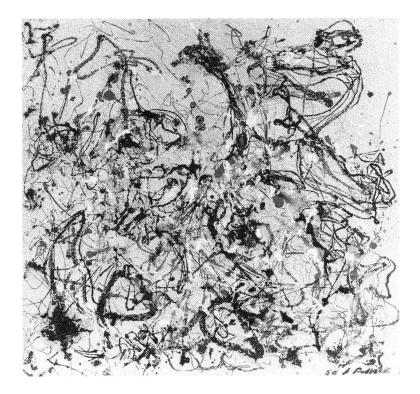

Jackson Pollock. *Number 16, 1950*. 1950.
Oil, duco, and aluminum paint on canvas. 22¼ × 22¼
inches (56.5 × 56.5 cm).
Museu de Arte Moderna, Rio de Janeiro, Brazil.

Franz Kline. *Corinthian*. 1957.
Oil on canvas. 80 × 120 inches (203.2 × 304.8 cm). Destroyed by fire, 1961.

version, *Corinthian, II*, 1961. By the following year, Kline, too, was dead.

In selecting contemporary American paintings, Nelson Rockefeller in no way limited his choices to Abstract Expressionism. He purchased works by many other Americans—again, shortly after they were painted. Among them were examples of Jasper Johns's long celebration of the alchemy of numbers, including one of his most eloquent. An early striped painting by Frank Stella and his heraldic tondo of 1968 were joined by hard-edged paintings by Fritz Glarner and Ellsworth Kelly, as well as by more disparate companions, such as Peter Dechar's inflated image, *Pear 68-11*, 1968, and Charles Hinman's three-dimensional shaped canvas.

Two of Nelson Rockefeller's architect friends helped him modify his house and apartment to accommodate more works of art. As the dining room in New York was being remodeled, Wallace Harrison suggested that it be redone completely with murals on the walls and ceiling—a practice more frequent in former times than today. This commission was entrusted to Glarner and resulted in an excellent environment. Philip Johnson, whom Nelson Rockefeller had first met in the 1930s, helped him add the space he needed for the recent works he was constantly acquiring. Mr. Johnson's solution was a long gallery, constructed at a lower level of the house at Pocantico Hills. The walls of his special room, almost 12 feet wide and 140 feet long, can accommodate large contemporary paintings and constructions. The gallery gradually descends underground, and opens—to a visitor's considerable astonishment—into a fantastic grotto, a splendid architectural folly of an older generation, which in turn opens onto a lower garden.

In sculpture, as in painting, Nelson Rockefeller's collection demonstrated his particular interest in advanced developments, particularly those of recent decades. However, he acquired a number of stellar works belonging to the previous fifty years, many of which have already been discussed. From the last decades of the nineteenth century, he owned three examples: two bronze studies by Auguste Rodin, and, by Aristide Maillol, the bronze *Bather Putting Up Her Hair*, enlarged to life size in 1930 from a small terra cotta of 1898. Two additional bronzes by Maillol, the pensive *Night* and the dynamic *Chained Action*, date from this century's first years. Although expressed in naturalistic terms, the underlying aesthetic of the latter work is not unlike that of Duchamp-Villon's *Horse*.

Nelson Rockefeller devoted particular attention to three American sculptors, each born before 1900, each highly individual in style: Gaston Lachaise and Elie Nadelman, both of whom left France to live in the United States, and Alexander Calder, an American who lived in France. At the Beaux-Arts in Paris, Lachaise had received a thorough academic training; and when he came to New York, he worked for a time as assistant to Paul Manship, a successful and highly favored sculptor who was the master of a somewhat lifeless pseudo-classic style. The exuberant vitality of Lachaise's art, however, was far removed from official taste. Obsessive deification of the opulent female form is central to his work. His heroic women overpower the spectator, and each dominating figure is, as well, a mother image. In spite of their often frank eroticism, these figures do not entice; they are idols, objects of awe.

Nelson Rockefeller had begun to collect bronzes by Lachaise before 1935, the year of the artist's death. Lachaise had also been among the artists commissioned for the decoration of Rockefeller Center. Mr. Rockefeller's interest in the sculptor's work continued, and in 1967 he bought the majestic *Standing Woman*, the most elegant of Lachaise's over-life-sized figures, which had been completed forty years before.

Born in Poland in 1882, the same year as Lachaise, Nadelman studied in Warsaw and Munich and worked for several years in France before arriving in the United States in 1914, shortly after the outbreak of the war. Original in style, he had been associated in Paris with the modern movement, in which he was influential, and numbered among his patrons Gertrude and Leo Stein. In New York, he soon established contact with the few Americans interested in advanced art, had a show at Stieglitz's "291" Gallery, and exhibited frequently thereafter, attaining considerable artistic and social success. During the last decades of his life, however, Nadelman became a recluse. He continued to produce but refused either to exhibit or sell. By the time of his death in 1946, he was almost forgotten. Nelson Rockefeller, however, remembered the artist well, and was particularly fond of his sculpture. He said: "He was a curious and wonderful man. My mother bought a great deal of her collection of American folk art

Aristide Maillol. *Chained Action: Torso of the Monument to Louis-Auguste Blanqui*. 1906.
Bronze. 47 inches (119.4 cm) high. NHT.

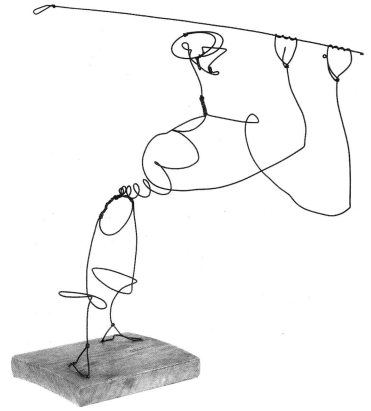

Alexander Calder. *The Golfer (John D. Rockefeller, Sr.).* c. 1928.
Wire construction. 15¼ × 9 × 12½ inches
(38.7 × 22.9 × 31.8 cm).

from the Nadelmans. . . . What interests me, . . . apart from the beauty and the wit of his pieces, is his very democratic concept of making many of his sculptures in *papier-mâché*, with the idea that they would be more financially available to the public."

Nelson Rockefeller owned some thirty of these doll-like, curiously proportioned figurines; they were scattered and constantly rearranged in his official residence in Albany, his house in Pocantico Hills, and his apartment in New York. He also collected several bronzes by Nadelman, of which the earliest was the *Standing Bull,* 1915, an intense work, aggressively modeled. The other bronzes are later in date and larger in size: a pair of relaxed seated "circus women," and two larger groups of two figures each, cast posthumously from originals in *papier-mâché.* Greatly enlarged versions of the latter two groups were also posthumously carved in marble for the Promenade of the New York State Theater in Lincoln Center. The attitudes of these graces are bemused, their forms soft and sometimes veiled, the surfaces ideally curved and sensuous.

Calder was a friend of Nelson Rockefeller for many years, and there were a number of Calders in his collection, among them two mobiles, of 1952 and 1962, and two stabiles, one an enlargement, over twelve feet high, of a small, perfect work cut and welded almost a quarter of a century before.

Yasuhide Kobashi. *Plumbob.* 1960.
White unglazed ceramic, wood frame, and nylon thread.
72 × 63¼ inches (182.9 × 160.9 cm).
Private collection.

Nelson Rockefeller particularly appreciated light-hearted humor and its rendering in three-dimensional objects. He owned several such pieces, usually in fragile mediums, and his associations with them were very personal. In his bedroom he kept a Calder drawing in wire, one of the artist's wittiest portraits of the late 1920s. Calder had mislaid this small caricature of John D. Rockefeller, Sr., as a golfer, but when he found it again in 1958, he gave it to the subject's grandson. Other objects, equally quick in their humor, included Isamu Noguchi's terra cotta *Mr. One-Man,* 1952, which sat on the governor's desk in Albany; and in his home in Pocantico Hills, an "arrange-it-yourself" of ceramic forms on strings by Yasuhide Kobashi, and two painted ceramic birds—an owl and a condor—by Picasso. A less intimate work, but similarly humorous, is Picasso's extraordinary group, *The Bathers,* which brings together six flat and angular mannequins, each cast in bronze from constructions assembled mostly of wood planks, with, paradoxically, as much insouciance as care.

In later years, sculpture was the most rapidly expanding part of Nelson Rockefeller's collection. He owned several classic and imposing examples in stone and bronze, which were traditionally carved or cast, by masters such as Arp, Moore, and Noguchi. Among these are two of Moore's great bronzes of the 1960s, *Knife Edge Two Piece,* one of the sculptor's most splendid achievements, and *Atom Piece,* the working model of the twelve-foot monument *Nuclear Energy,* commissioned for the site on the campus of the University of Chicago where the atom was first split in underground laboratories (now destroyed). Noguchi's *Black Sun,* carved in granite, was also enlarged to monumental scale and occupies a site in front of the art museum in Seattle, Washington.

Tony Smith. *Wandering Rocks*. 1967.
Stainless steel, vapor-blasted. Five pieces: dud, 22½ × 98 × 31 inches (57.2 × 248.9 × 78.8 cm);
slide, 22½ × 76 × 27½ inches (57.2 × 193 × 69.9 cm); crocus, 47 × 45 × 27 inches (119.4 ×
114.3 × 68.1 cm); shaft, 72 × 45 × 27½ inches (182.9 × 114.3 × 69.9 cm); smohawk,
27½ × 47 × 22½ inches (69.9 × 119.4 × 57.2 cm).
NHT.

Increasingly, Nelson Rockefeller sought works by sculptors whose reputations had developed more recently, and who did not hesitate to work with less conventional materials. Some of these works are of extraordinary size, and of a scale that commands much space for their installation. An extreme example is the five-part *Wandering Rocks* by Tony Smith which, like Clement Meadmore's *U Turn*, is almost a landscape in itself.

American sculpture was particularly well represented in the collection. There were two masterpieces in steel by David Smith: one of his "drawings in space," *The Banquet*, 1951, and the huge *Voltri VI*, one of the prolific series welded in Italy in 1962. In some respects, Smith's sculpture parallels the painting of the Abstract Expressionists, as do, still more closely, works by other artists: Herbert Ferber, in copper; Ibram Lassaw, in lead over copper; and two pieces, of steel and other metals, by Seymour Lipton—*The Cloak*, 1952, a vertical and visceral metaphor, and the *Storm Bird*, 1953, a horizontal creature, alert and poised for flight. The sculptor Louise Nevelson might also be considered a counterpart to the Abstract Expressionist painters, especially in such a work as the white, painted wood construction, two parts of a larger assemblage originally designed to fill a

Seymour Lipton. *Storm Bird*. 1953.
Welded nickel silver over steel. 20 × 37 × 9⅝
inches (50.8 × 94 × 24.5 cm).
Private collection.

45

Francesco Somaini. *Wounded, III*. 1960.
Cast iron with iron base. 13 × 17¼ × 14 inches
(33 × 43.8 × 35.6 cm).
NHT.

Robert Mallary. *Head of a Bull*. 1958.
Relief: composition stone in resin base. 33 × 33 inches
(83.8 × 83.8 cm).
NHT.

Larry Bell. Untitled *(14-C)*. 1966–67.
Tinted glass with chrome mounting on Plexiglas
pedestal. 14½-inch (36.6-cm) cube; pedestal,
43 inches (109.2 cm) high.
NHT.

room. Nevelson was also represented in the collection by two more recent architectonic constructions, an aluminum wall and a small Plexiglas object, which invite the eye to penetrate their laddered open spaces.

Among the other American sculptors in the collection were three whose works, in conception and execution, stand somewhat apart from their American contemporaries. The shimmering, linear tension of Richard Lippold's taut *Bird of Paradise* in gold offers a complete contrast to Raoul Hague's *Annandale-on-Hudson*, carved of solid walnut. Robert Mallary's *Head of a Bull* expressively lends to humble materials, composition stone and resin, a poetry that is lonely, tragic, and abandoned.

Younger American sculptors in the collection worked in even more varied mediums and in more recent modes of expression. Larry Bell and Lee Bontecou each created completely different abstract poems—the former a delicately tinted, precisely designed glass cube, the other a canvas and metal construction with a mysterious, asymmetrically placed round aperture. Less concerned with mood are the welded sculptures of Jason Seley and Richard Stankiewicz, which transform scrap metal into elegant assemblages, and a remarkable piece, *Granny's Knot*, by Shinkichi Tajiri.

Although Nelson Rockefeller's collection of contemporary sculpture represented his personal choice and made no attempt to be comprehensive, it was nevertheless a broad international selection. Among the many works by foreign artists, for example, were those by four British sculptors younger than Moore—Kenneth Armitage, Reg Butler, Lynn Chadwick, and Eduardo Paolozzi; by three Italian sculptors, Umberto Mastroianni, Arnaldo Pomodoro, and Francesco Somaini; by Masayuke Nagare of Japan; and by artists resident in Paris—Pol Bury, Horst Egon Kalinowski, and Jean Ipousteguy; as well as many others.

In private and in public life, the man who owned these works of art ran counter to the tradition set by most American statesmen. As a connoisseur, he was thoroughly acquainted with the broad span of modern art; he was also a champion of his own time and of the future. As a collector, he was determined and audacious. He knew that what he needed from himself was an immediate response; he was interested in what a work looked like, not what it represented. Once acquired, the work was subjected to constant scrutiny, as he studied its construction, pattern, and formal relationships.

Nelson Rockefeller was never so happy and relaxed as when he acted as his own curator, hanging paintings or placing sculpture. Whenever he installed, he insisted on touching and physically moving the object himself, often to his associates' dismay. In addition, he was by far the most

Umberto Mastroianni. *The Sun*. 1961. Bronze. 50⅞ × 4⅛ × 30 inches (128.9 × 10.5 × 76.2 cm). NHT.

eloquent docent for his own collection, as those who have heard him can testify.

The collection, considered as a general survey of modern art, naturally had some fascinating omissions because the choice of treasures was so personal. But it was one of the most glorious ever assembled.

47

PLATES

Auguste Rodin. *The Age of Bronze (The Vanquished)*. 1875–76.
Bronze. 41¼ inches (104.8 cm) high.

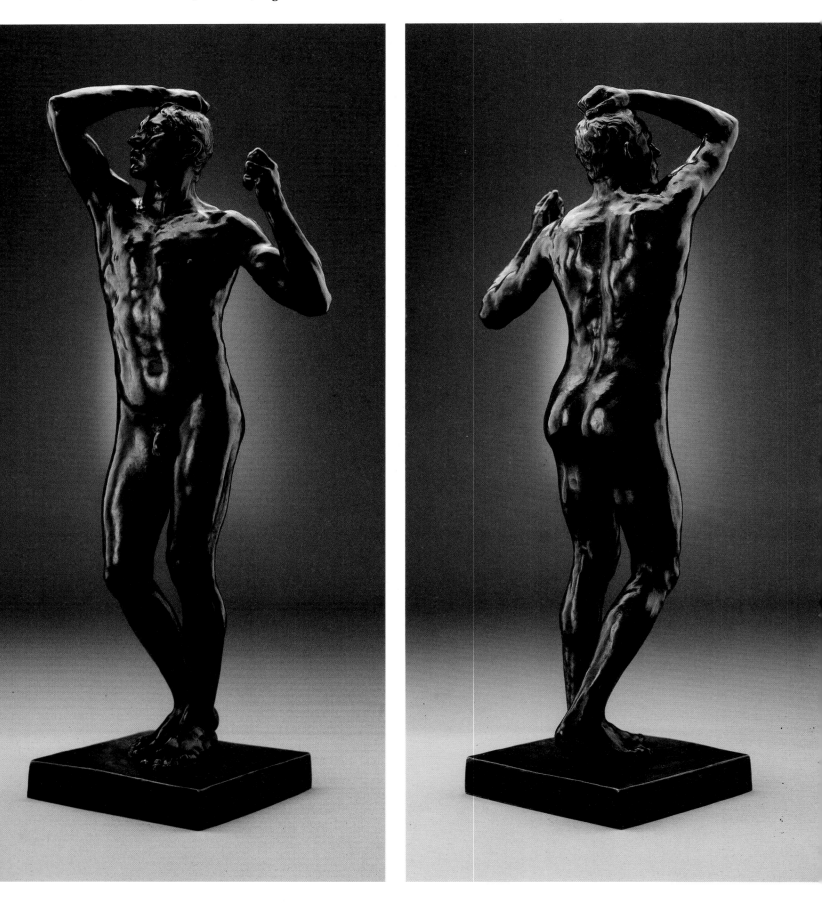

Auguste Rodin. *Torso of Adele*. c. 1882.
Bronze. 18 × 7½ × 6 inches (45.7 × 19.1 × 15.2 cm).
NHT.

Aristide Maillol. *Night*. 1902–09 (this cast after 1944).
Bronze. 41½ × 40⅝ × 24 inches (105.4 × 103.2 × 61 cm).
NHT.

Left
Aristide Maillol. *Bather Putting Up Her Hair*. 1930 (after a small figure of 1898).
Bronze. 61½ inches (156.2 cm) high.
NHT.

Pablo Picasso. *Study for The Actor* (with two profiles of Fernande). 1904–05.
Pencil on paper. 19 × 12½ inches (48.3 × 31.8 cm).
Collection Mr. and Mrs. Sidney E. Cohn.

Pablo Picasso. Sheet of studies: *Figures and Bulls*. 1905.
Pen and ink on paper. 13⅛ × 10¼ inches (33.5 × 26 cm).
Private collection.

Right
Pablo Picasso. *Woman Combing Her Hair*. 1906.
Bronze. 16⅝ inches (42.2 cm) high.
Private collection.
This cast: The Baltimore Museum of Art, The Cone
Collection, formed by Dr. Claribel Cone and Miss Etta
Cone of Baltimore, Maryland.

Elie Nadelman. *Standing Bull*. 1915.
Bronze. 6⅝ × 11¼ inches (16.8 × 28.6 cm).
NHT.

Left
Constantin Brancusi. *The Kiss*. After 1908–10 (after a stone original of 1907–08).
Plaster. 11 × 10¼ × 8⅝ inches (27.9 × 26 × 21.9 cm).
Latner and Envoy Family Collection.

Maurice de Vlaminck. *The Woodcutter (The Chestnut Grove at La Jonchère)*. 1905.
Oil on canvas. 29 × 36 inches (73.7 × 91.4 cm).
Private collection.

Wassily Kandinsky. *Autumn Landscape, Murnau*. 1908.
Oil on composition board. 27¼ × 37¼ inches (69.2 × 94.6 cm) (sight).
Bequeathed to The Museum of Modern Art, New York.

Albert Marquet. *Ciboure*. 1907.
Oil on canvas. 16¼ × 13½ inches (41.3 × 34.3 cm).
Private collection.

Below

Alexey Jawlensky. *Cottage in the Woods*. 1903.
Oil on wood. 20¼ × 19¼ inches (51.4 × 48.9 cm).

Alexey Jawlensky. *The Spanish Girl*. 1912.
Oil on paper, mounted on cardboard. 27 × 19¼ inches (68.6 × 48.9 cm).
Private collection, Germany.

Wilhelm Lehmbruck. *Meditating Girl*. 1911.
Terra cotta. 21 inches (53.3 cm) high.

Wilhelm Lehmbruck. *Dancer*. 1913–14.
Cast stone. 11½ inches (29.2 cm) high.
The Museum of Modern Art, New York.
Nelson A. Rockefeller Bequest.

Right
Wilhelm Lehmbruck. *Torso*. 1910.
Cast stone. 45 inches (114.3 cm) high.

Henri Matisse. *Reclining Nude, I.* 1907.
Bronze. 13½ × 19¾ × 9⅜ inches (34.3 × 50.2 × 23.8 cm).
Private collection, New York.

Right
Henri Matisse. *Seated Nude.* 1925.
Bronze. 31½ × 29⅝ × 13¾ inches (80 × 75.2 × 35 cm).
Thyssen-Bornèmisza Collection.

Henri Matisse. *View of Collioure and the Sea*. 1911.
Oil on canvas. 24¾ × 20⅜ inches (62.9 × 51.8 cm).
The Museum of Modern Art, New York. Nelson A. Rockefeller Bequest.

Henri Matisse. *Italian Woman*. 1915.
Oil on canvas. 45¾ × 35¼ inches (116.2 × 89.5 cm).
The Museum of Modern Art, New York. Gift of Nelson A. Rockefeller.

Amedeo Modigliani. *The Dreamer*. 1918.
Oil on canvas. 23½ × 36¼ inches (59.7 × 92.1 cm).
Private collection.

Left
Kees van Dongen. *Woman in a Large Hat*. 1908.
Oil on canvas. 39½ × 32 inches (100.3 × 81.3 cm).
The Museum of Modern Art, New York. Nelson A. Rockefeller Bequest.

Giorgio de Chirico. *The Song of Love*. 1914.
Oil on canvas. 28¾ × 23⅜ inches (73 × 59.4 cm).
The Museum of Modern Art, New York. Nelson A. Rockefeller Bequest.

Constantin Brancusi. *Bird in Space*. c. 1923–41
(this cast 1970).
Bronze. 72¾ inches (184.9 cm) high.
NHT.

Pablo Picasso. *Head*. 1907.
Watercolor and gouache on
paper, mounted on panel.
12⅛ × 9⅜ inches (30.8 ×
23.8 cm).
Collection Mr. and Mrs.
Sidney E. Cohn.

Pablo Picasso. *Head*. 1907.
Tempera and watercolor on
paper, mounted on panel.
12¼ × 9½ inches (31.1 ×
24.1 cm).
Private collection, England.

Pablo Picasso. *Kneeling Woman (Study for Three Women)*. 1908. Charcoal on paper. 25 × 18⅜ inches (63.5 × 46.6 cm). Collection Mr. and Mrs. Jacques Gelman, New York.

Pablo Picasso. *Glasses and Fruits*. 1908. Oil on wood. 10⅝ × 8¼ inches (27 × 21 cm). Thyssen-Bornemisza Collection.

Pablo Picasso. *Houses on the Hill, Horta de Ebro*. 1909.
Oil on canvas. 25 ⅝ × 31 ⅞ inches (65.2 × 81 cm).
The Museum of Modern Art, New York. Nelson A. Rockefeller Bequest.

Right
Pablo Picasso. *Girl with a Mandolin (Fanny Tellier)*. 1910.
Oil on canvas. 39 ½ × 29 inches (100.3 × 73.6 cm).
The Museum of Modern Art, New York. Nelson A. Rockefeller Bequest.

Pablo Picasso. *Still Life: Le Torero*. 1911.
Oil on canvas. 18 ¼ × 15 ⅛ inches (46.4 × 38.4 cm).
Bequeathed to The Museum of Modern Art, New York.

Pablo Picasso. *Guitar*. 1913.
Charcoal, crayon, ink, and pasted paper.
26 ⅛ × 19 ½ inches (66.3 × 49.5 cm).
The Museum of Modern Art, New York.
Nelson A. Rockefeller Bequest.

Georges Braque. *Clarinet*. 1913.
Pasted papers, charcoal, chalk, and oil on canvas. 37½ × 47⅜ inches (95.2 × 120.3 cm).
The Museum of Modern Art, New York. Nelson A. Rockefeller Bequest.

Pablo Picasso. *Study for Guitar on a Table*. 1912–13.
Charcoal on paper. 25 × 19⅛ inches (63.5 × 48.6 cm).
Private collection.

Pablo Picasso. *Guitar on a Table*. 1912–13.
Oil, charcoal, and sand on canvas. 24¼ × 20⅛ inches (61.6 × 51.1 cm).
Dartmouth College Museum and Galleries, Hanover, New Hampshire.

Pablo Picasso. *Student with a Pipe*. 1913–14.
Oil, charcoal, pasted paper, and sand on canvas. 28¾ × 23⅛ inches (73 × 58.7 cm).
The Museum of Modern Art, New York. Nelson A. Rockefeller Bequest.

Albert Gleizes. *Football Players*. 1912–13.
Oil on canvas. 89 × 72 inches (226.2 × 183 cm).
National Gallery of Art, Washington, D.C. Ailsa Mellon Bruce Fund.

Right
Raymond Duchamp-Villon. *The Horse (Le Cheval majeur)*. 1914
(this cast 1966).
Bronze. 59 × 35½ × 53½ inches (149.9 × 90.2 × 135.9 cm).
NHT.

Georges Braque. *Guitar, Newspaper, and Bottle*. 1913–14.
Oil on canvas. 28⅞ × 21¼ inches (73.4 × 54 cm).
Private collection.

Right
Juan Gris. *Guitar, Bottle, and Glass*. 1914.
Pasted papers, gouache, and crayon on canvas.
36⅛ × 25½ inches (91.8 × 64.8 cm).
The Museum of Modern Art, New York.
Nelson A. Rockefeller Bequest.

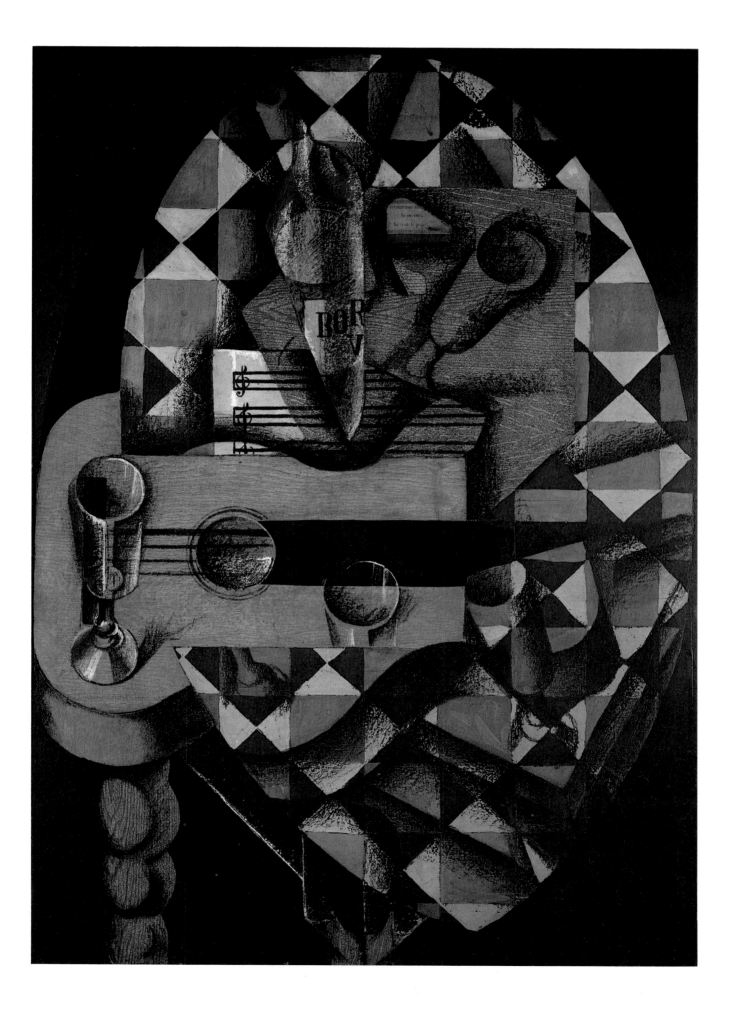

Pablo Picasso. *Still Life: "Job."* 1916.
Oil and sand on canvas. 17 × 13¼ inches (43.2 × 33.7 cm).
The Museum of Modern Art, New York. Nelson A. Rockefeller Bequest.

Juan Gris. *The Sideboard*. 1917.
Oil on plywood. 45⅞ × 28¾ inches (116.5 × 73 cm).
The Museum of Modern Art, New York. Nelson A. Rockefeller Bequest.

Umberto Boccioni. *States of Mind: Those Who Go*. 1911.
Oil on canvas. 27⅞ × 38 inches (70.8 × 96.5 cm).
The Museum of Modern Art, New York. Gift of Nelson A. Rockefeller.

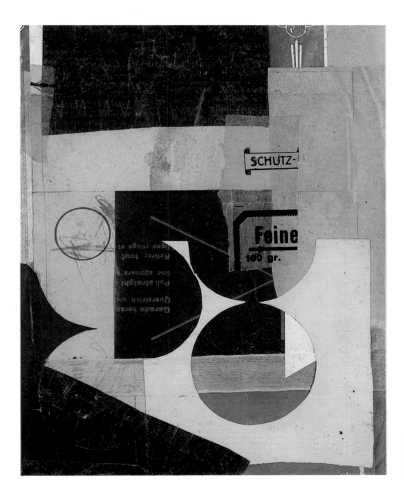
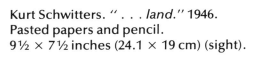

Kurt Schwitters. *Merz 430: "Feine 100 gr."* 1922.
Pasted papers and ribbon.
8½ × 6¾ inches (21.6 × 17.1 cm) (sight).

Kurt Schwitters. *" . . . land."* 1946.
Pasted papers and pencil.
9½ × 7½ inches (24.1 × 19 cm) (sight).

Umberto Boccioni. *States of Mind: Those Who Stay*. 1911.
Oil on canvas. 27 ¾ × 37 ⅜ inches (70.5 × 95 cm).
The Museum of Modern Art, New York. Gift of Nelson A. Rockefeller.

Umberto Boccioni. *States of Mind: The Farewells*. 1911.
Oil on canvas. 27¾ × 37⅞ inches (70.5 × 96.2 cm).
The Museum of Modern Art, New York. Gift of Nelson A. Rockefeller.

Piet Mondrian. *Large Composition A*. 1920.
Oil on canvas. 35½ × 35¾ inches (90.2 × 90.8 cm).
Galleria Nazionale d'Arte Moderna, Rome.

Jacques Lipchitz. *Seated Man with Guitar*. 1922.
Basalt. 15⅞ inches (40.2 cm) high.

Alexander Archipenko. *Standing Woman*. 1923
(possibly after a terra cotta of c. 1920).
Mahogany. 17½ inches (44.4 cm).
Private collection.

Fernand Léger. *Woman with a Book*. 1923.
Oil on canvas. 45¾ × 32⅛ inches (116.2 × 81.5 cm).
The Museum of Modern Art, New York. Nelson A. Rockefeller Bequest.

Right
Jacques Lipchitz. *Song of the Vowels*. 1931–32 (this cast 1952–53). Bronze. 119 × 82 inches (302.5 × 208.3 cm).
NHT.

Georges Braque. *The Table*. 1930.
Oil and sand on canvas. 57⅝ × 30⅜ inches (146.4 × 77.2 cm).
Bequeathed to The Museum of Modern Art, New York.

Georg Kolbe. *Grief*. 1921.
Bronze. 15¾ × 22 inches (40 × 55.9 cm).

Below

Georg Kolbe. *The Call of the Earth*. 1932.
Bronze. 28½ inches (72.4 cm) high.
NHT.

Right

Gerhard Marcks. *Maja*. 1942.
Bronze. 89 inches (226.1 cm) high.
NHT.

Gaston Lachaise. *Torso*. 1932.
Bronze. 7⅝ inches (19.4 cm) high.

Below
Gaston Lachaise. *Couple (Dans la nuit)*. 1935.
Bronze. 31 × 88½ × 41 inches
(78.8 × 224.8 × 104.1 cm).
NHT.

Gaston Lachaise. *Standing Woman (Elevation)*. 1912–27 (this cast 1967).
Bronze. 70½ inches (179.1 cm) high.
NHT.

Elie Nadelman. *Two Nudes*. c. 1931 (this cast 1949).
Bronze. 59 inches (149.9 cm) high.
NHT.

Right
Elie Nadelman. *Two Circus Women*. c. 1930 (this cast 1951).
Bronze. 61 ¼ inches (155.6 cm) high.
NHT.

Elie Nadelman. *Circus Woman, II.* c. 1924 (this cast 1965).
Bronze. 44¾ inches (113.6 cm) high.

Pablo Picasso. *Figure Study, Back*. 1920–21.
Charcoal on gray paper. 24¾ × 18¾ inches (62.9 × 47.6 cm).
Private collection, Germany.

Pablo Picasso. *Study of a Hand*. 1921.
Pastel on paper.
8¼ × 12⅝ inches (21 × 32.1 cm).
Private collection.

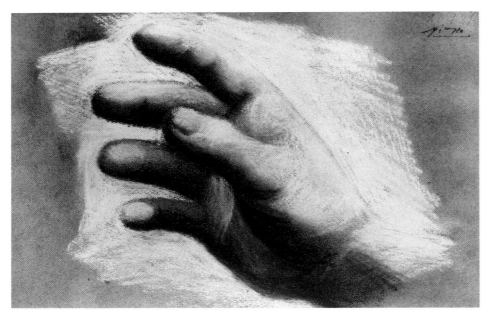

Pablo Picasso. *Red and White Owl*. 1953.
Painted ceramic. 13¾ inches (35 cm) high.
Collection Mr. and Mrs. Thomas B. Morgan.

Pablo Picasso. *Condor*. 1949.
Painted ceramic. 13 × 13½ inches
(33 × 34.3 cm).

Pablo Picasso. *Pitcher and Bowl of Fruit*. 1931.
Oil on canvas. 51¼ × 63¾ inches (130.2 × 162 cm).
The Museum of Modern Art, New York. Nelson A. Rockefeller Bequest.

Pablo Picasso. *Interior with a Girl Drawing*. 1935.
Oil on canvas. 51¼ × 76⅝ inches (130.2 × 194.6 cm).
The Museum of Modern Art, New York. Nelson A. Rockefeller Bequest.

Pablo Picasso. *Portrait of D.M.* 1939.
Oil on canvas. 36⅛ × 25⅝ inches (91.7 × 65.1 cm).
Private collection.

Pablo Picasso. *The Striped Bodice*. 1943.
Oil on canvas. 39¼ × 32 inches (99.6 × 82 cm).
The Museum of Modern Art, New York. Gift of Nelson A. Rockefeller.

Right

Pablo Picasso. *The Bathers*. 1956.
Bronze (after carved wood). Six figures: bather, 104 × 33⅜ inches
(264.1 × 84.8 cm); man with joined hands, 96¾ × 32½ inches
(254.8 × 82.5 cm); fountain man, 84¼ × 25⅝ inches
(214 × 65.1 cm); diver, 78½ × 69 inches (199.4 ×
175.3 cm); bather, 69¾ × 19½ inches (177.1 × 49.5 cm);
head, 53½ × 27 inches (135.9 × 68.6 cm).
NHT.

Julio Gonzalez. *Reclining Figure*. 1934.
Wrought iron. 18 × 37 × 16¾ inches (45.7 × 94 × 42.5 cm).
The Museum of Modern Art, New York. Nelson A. Rockefeller Bequest.

Pablo Picasso. *Woman and Dwarf*. 1953.
Brush and ink on paper.
13¾ × 10⅜ inches (35 × 26.4 cm).

Below
Pablo Picasso. *The Models, III*. 1954.
Brush and ink on paper.
9½ × 12⅝ inches (24 × 32 cm).
Private collection.

Pablo Picasso. *The Studio Visit, IV*. 1954.
Brush and ink on paper. 9½ × 12⅝ inches (23.8 × 32.1 cm).
Private collection.

Pablo Picasso. *Models Posing*. 1954.
Brush and ink on paper. 9⅜ × 12½ inches (23.8 × 31.8 cm).
Private collection.

Paul Klee. *Yellow Harbor*. 1921.
Pen and ink, transfer process, watercolor, and wash on paper.
12¼ × 19 inches (31.8 × 48.3 cm).
Private collection, Switzerland.

Paul Klee. *Sharp Profile*. 1924.
Pen and ink, transfer process, and wash on paper.
10 × 11¼ inches (25.4 × 28.6 cm).
Private collection, Switzerland.

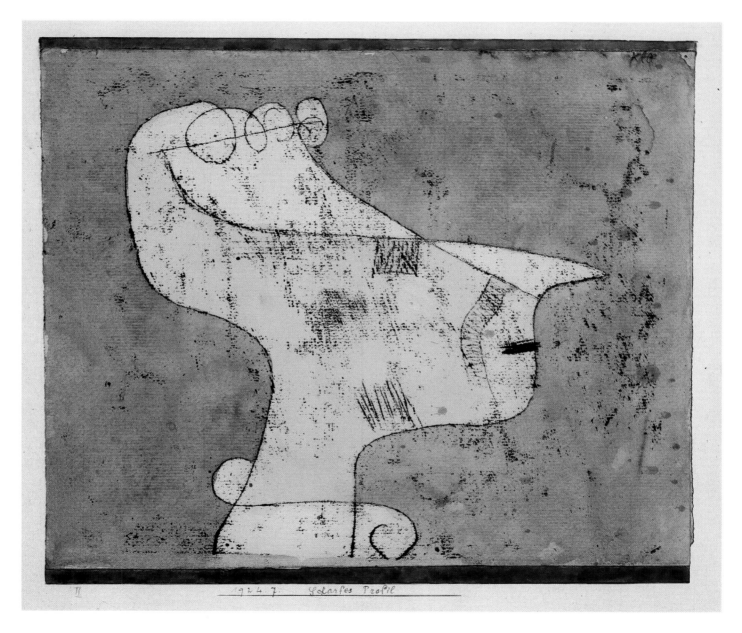

Paul Klee. *The Wall, I*. 1929.
Watercolor and wash on paper. 18 × 10¼ inches (45.7 × 26 cm).

Paul Klee. *Prince*. 1930.
Pen and ink and watercolor on pink paper.
18¾ × 12½ inches (47.6 × 31.8 cm).

Paul Klee. *Fear.* 1934.
Oil on burlap. 19¾ × 21¼ inches (50.2 × 55.3 cm).
The Museum of Modern Art, New York. Nelson A. Rockefeller Fund.

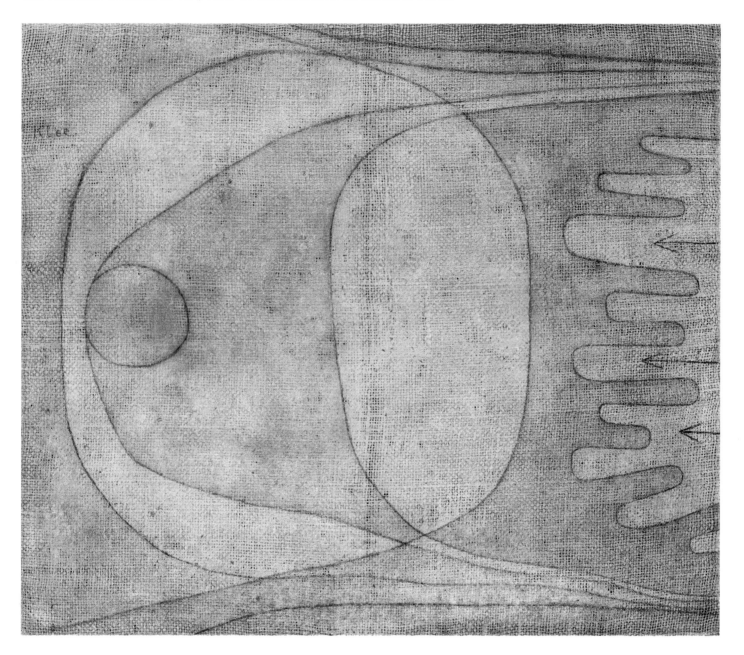

Right
Paul Klee. *Heroic Strokes of the Bow (Heroische Bogenstriche).* 1938.
Tempera on paper, on cloth with gesso backing.
28¾ × 20⅞ inches (73 × 53 cm).
The Museum of Modern Art, New York. Nelson A. Rockefeller Bequest.

119

Joan Miró. *Seated Woman*. 1935.
Oil on cardboard, mounted on canvas. 29⅝ × 41⅝ inches (75.2 × 105.7 cm).
Galleria Nazionale d'Arte Moderna, Rome.

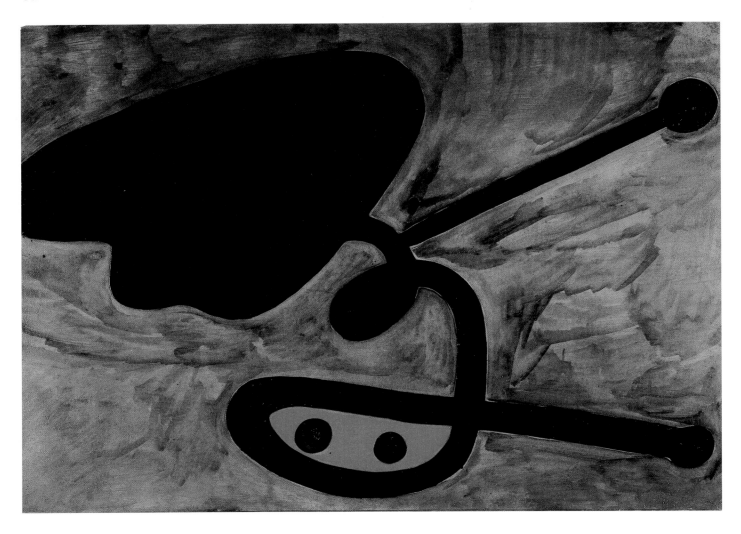

Right
Joan Miró. *Collage*. 1933.
Pasted papers, charcoal, pencil, and ink on sandpaper, mounted
on canvas. 42¾ × 28⅛ inches (108.6 × 71.4 cm).

Joan Miró. *Painting, 1933*. 1933.
Oil on canvas. 51¼ × 77 inches (130.2 × 195.6 cm).
Private collection.

Joan Miró. *Hirondelle/Amour*. 1933–34.
Oil on canvas. 78½ × 97½ inches (199.3 × 247.6 cm).
The Museum of Modern Art, New York. Gift of Nelson A. Rockefeller.

Joan Miró. *Woman and Bird Before the Moon*. 1944.
Oil, pastel, and gouache on canvas. 7½ × 4½ inches (19.1 ×
10.8 cm).

Jean Arp. *Man with a Moustache*. c. 1924.
Oil on cardboard with cut-outs. 21⅝ × 19½ inches (54.9 × 49.5 cm).
Private collection.

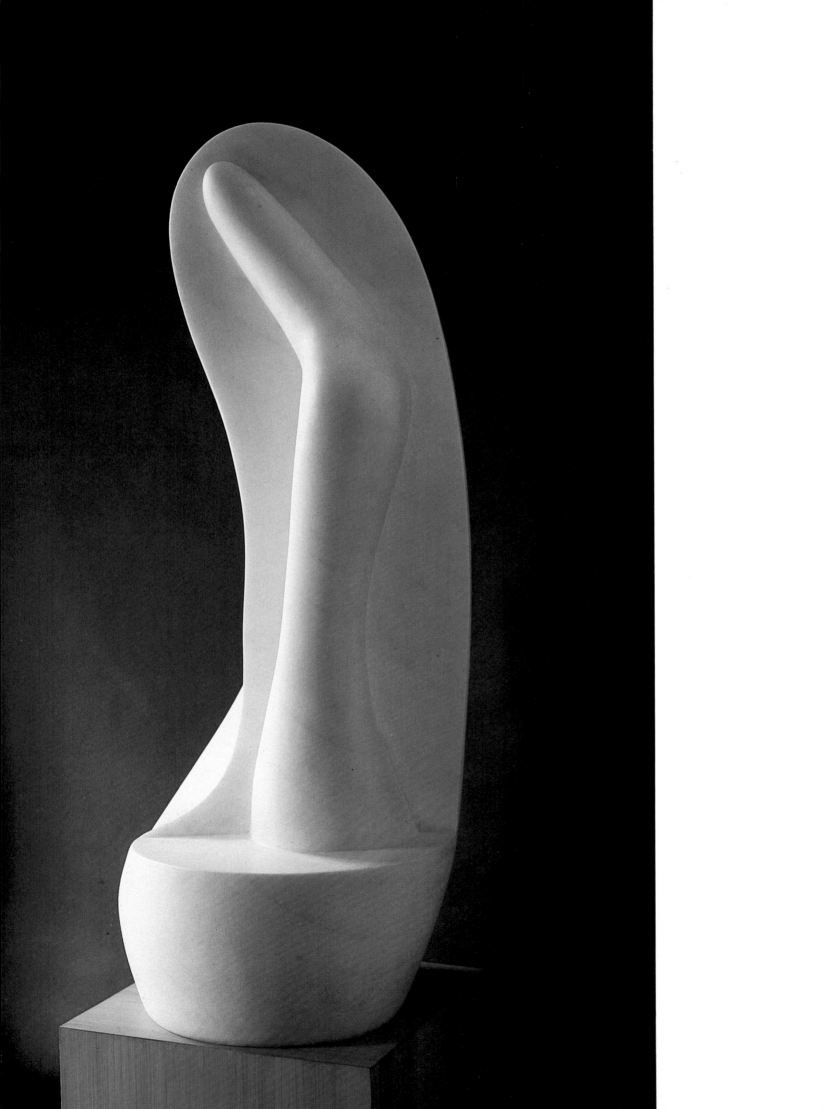

Left
Jean Arp. *Amphora of the Muse*. 1959.
Marble. 44¾ inches (113.7 cm) high.

Jean Arp. *Shell Crystal*. 1938.
Black fossiliferous limestone. 13 × 14¾ × 13 inches
(33 × 37.5 × 33 cm).

Jean Arp. *Snake Movement, II*. 1955.
Concrete. 16¼ × 28 × 23¼ inches (41.3 × 71.1 × 59 cm).
NHT.

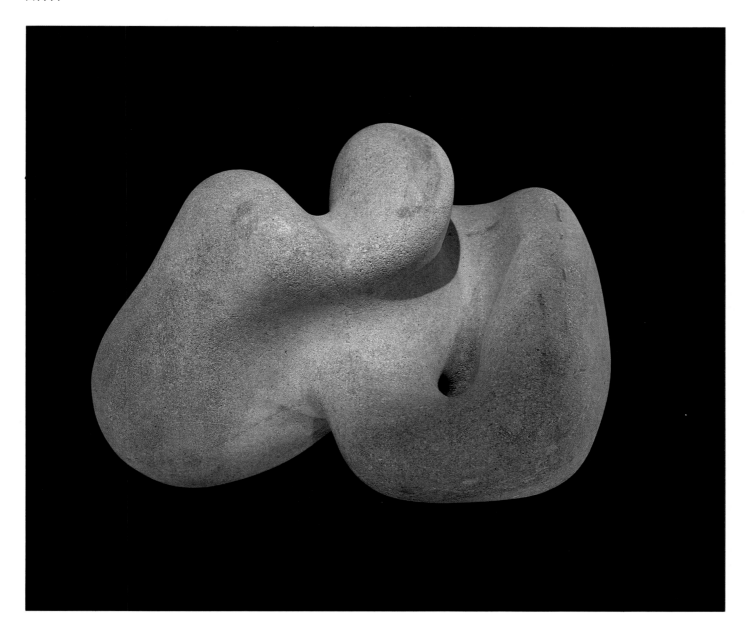

Left
Alberto Giacometti. *Spoon Woman*. 1926.
Bronze. 57 inches (144.8 cm) high.
Collection Mr. and Mrs. Burton Tremaine, Meriden, Connecticut.

Alberto Giacometti. *Woman with Her Throat Cut*. 1932 (this cast 1950).
Bronze. 8 × 34½ × 25 inches (20.3 × 87.6 × 63.5 cm).
National Galleries of Scotland, Edinburgh.

Alberto Giacometti. *City Square (La Place)*. 1948.
Bronze. 8½ × 25⅜ × 17¼ inches (21.6 × 64.5 × 43.8 cm).
Private collection.
This cast: The Museum of Modern Art, New York.

Alberto Giacometti. *Walking Quickly Under the Rain*. 1949.
Bronze. 17⅝ × 32 × 6 inches (44.8 × 81.3 × 15.2 cm).

Left
Alberto Giacometti. *Nude*. 1932–36 (this cast 1960).
Bronze. 58 × 10⅜ inches (147.3 × 26.4 cm).
NHT.

Georges Rouault. *The Judge*. 1930.
Ink, wash, and pastel on paper. 22¾ × 16¾ inches (57.8 × 42.5 cm).
Collection John C. Whitehead, New York.

Right
Max Beckmann. *Woman with a Parrot*. 1946.
Oil on canvas. 37¼ × 23¾ inches (94.6 × 60.3 cm).
Collection Mr. and Mrs. Joel Honigberg, Chicago.

Giorgio Morandi. *Still Life*. 1939.
Oil on canvas. 17⅛ × 20¾ inches (43.5 × 52.7 cm).
Private collection.

Lyonel Feininger. *The Burglar*. 1903.
Pen and ink and gouache on paper. 5½ × 8⅝ inches (14 × 21.9 cm)

Charles Demuth. *Bouquet*. c. 1923.
Watercolor on paper. 17⅝ × 11⅝ inches (44.8 × 29.5 cm) (sight).
Private collection.

Alexander Calder. *Large Spiny*. 1966
(after the stabile of 1942).
Stabile: painted sheet steel. 150 × 210 ×
102 inches (381.2 × 533.7 × 259.6 cm).

Alexander Calder. *Black Sickles, Black Commas*. 1962.
Mobile: painted sheet metal and steel rod. 34 × 68 inches (86.5 × 72.5 cm).

Left

Alexander Calder. *Mobile in Black and Silver*. 1952.
Sheet aluminum and steel rod, on painted sheet steel base.
c. 180 inches (457.5 cm) high.
Collection Martin Z. Margulies, Miami, Florida.

Alexander Calder. *Cattails and Bird*. 1968.
Gouache on paper. 43⅛ × 29⅜ inches (109.5 × 74.6 cm).

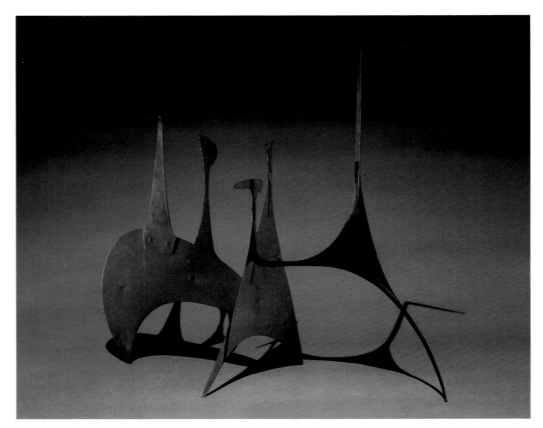

Alexander Calder. *Spiny*. 1942.
Stabile: painted sheet aluminum. 26 × 30 × 14⅜ inches
(66 × 76.2 × 36.5 cm).
The Museum of Modern Art, New York. Nelson A. Rockefeller Bequest.

Henry Moore. *Family Group*. 1948–49 (this cast 1951).
Bronze. 59¼ × 46½ inches (150.5 × 118 cm).
Hakone Open-Air Museum, Kanagawa-Ken, Japan.

Henry Moore. Maquette for *King and Queen*. 1952.
Bronze. 10¾ × 8¼ inches (27.3 × 21 cm).

Henry Moore. *Rocking Chair, I*. 1950.
Bronze. 12⅛ × 3⅞ × 10½ inches
(30.8 × 9.8 × 26.7 cm).

Henry Moore. Maquette for *Double Oval*. 1966.
Bronze. 7⅛ × 9½ inches (18.1 × 24 cm).

Henry Moore. *Reclining Figure, I*. 1945.
Bronze. 15 inches (38.1 cm) long.

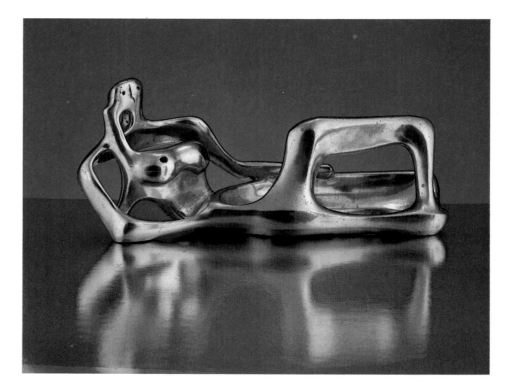

Henry Moore. *Atom Piece* (Working model for *Nuclear Energy*). 1964–65.
Bronze. 45½ × 28 × 27 inches (115.6 × 71.1 × 68 cm).
NHT.

Henry Moore. *Knife Edge Two Piece*. 1962 (large version 1965–66).
Bronze. 104 × 139 × 44 inches (264.5 × 353 × 112 cm).
NHT.

Reg Butler. *Oracle*. 1952 (this cast 1956).
Cast shell bronze welded to forged bronze armature.
33½ × 73 × 35½ inches (85.1 × 184.4 × 90.2 cm).
NHT.

Naum Gabo. *Construction in Space, X.* 1953.
Plexiglas, nylon wire, and aluminum. 28¾ × 18⅛ × 18⅝
inches (73 × 46 × 47.3 cm); base: ⅞ × 13¼ × 21¾ inches
(2.2 × 33.7 × 55.2 cm).
The Museum of Modern Art, New York. Nelson A. Rockefeller Bequest.

Fritz Glarner. *Relational Painting, Tondo 36.* 1954–55.
Oil on composition board. 41 inches (104.1 cm) diameter.
Andre Emmerich Gallery, New York and Zurich.

Wifredo Lam. *Chemical Nuptials*. 1944.
Oil and charcoal on canvas. 61¾ × 49¾ inches (156.8 × 126.4 cm).
Private collection.

Diego Rivera. *The Balcony*. 1921.
Encaustic on canvas. 32 × 25⅝ inches (81.3 × 61.5 cm).
Collection Samuel Goldwyn, Jr.

Peter Blume. *Excavation*. 1945.
Oil on canvas. 21⅛ × 27 inches (53.7 × 68.6 cm).

Julio Castellanos. *St. John's Day*. 1938.
Oil on canvas. 15¾ × 18⅞ inches (40 × 48 cm).
Private collection.

Paul Delvaux. *The Watchman, II*. 1961.
Oil on composition board. 48 × 96 inches (121.4 × 244 cm).
Nationalgalerie, Berlin.

Paul Delvaux. *The Mirage*. 1967.
Watercolor and ink on paper. 24⅜ × 39⅛ inches (61.9 × 99.4 cm).
NHT.

Karel Appel. *Bird Woman*. 1951.
Oil on canvas. 57¼ × 38⅛ inches (145.4 × 96.8 cm).
NHT.

Arshile Gorky. *The Calendars*. 1946–47.
Oil on canvas. 50 × 60 inches (127 × 152.4 cm).
Destroyed by fire, 1961.

Right
Frederick J. Kiesler. *Galaxy*. 1951.
Wood construction. 144 inches (365.8 cm) high; dimensions
around base: 156 × 138 × 130 inches (396.2 × 350.5 × 330.2 cm).

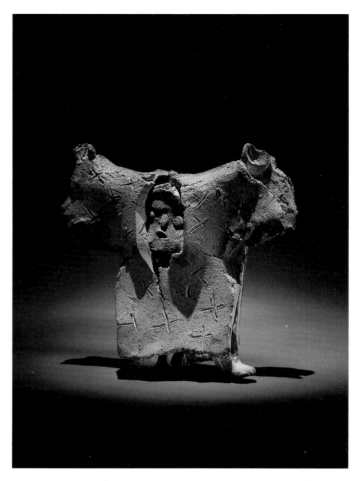

Isamu Noguchi. *Celebration*. 1952.
Cast iron. 17 7/8 × 21 × 1 3/8 inches (45.4 × 53.3 × 3.5 cm).

Right above
Isamu Noguchi. *Small Child*. 1952.
Ceramic (karatzu ware). 6 1/4 × 6 1/4 inches (15.9 × 15.9 cm).

Right
Isamu Noguchi. *Mr. One-Man*. 1952.
Ceramic (kasama ware). 11 1/4 × 9 7/8 × 8 1/2 inches (28.6 × 25.1 × 21.6 cm).

Far right
Isamu Noguchi. *Abstract Sculpture*. 1947.
White marble. 76 1/2 inches (194.3 cm) high.
Norton Simon Museum, Pasadena, California.
Purchased with the aid of funds from
the National Endowment
for the Arts and the Fellows Acquisition Fund, 1974.

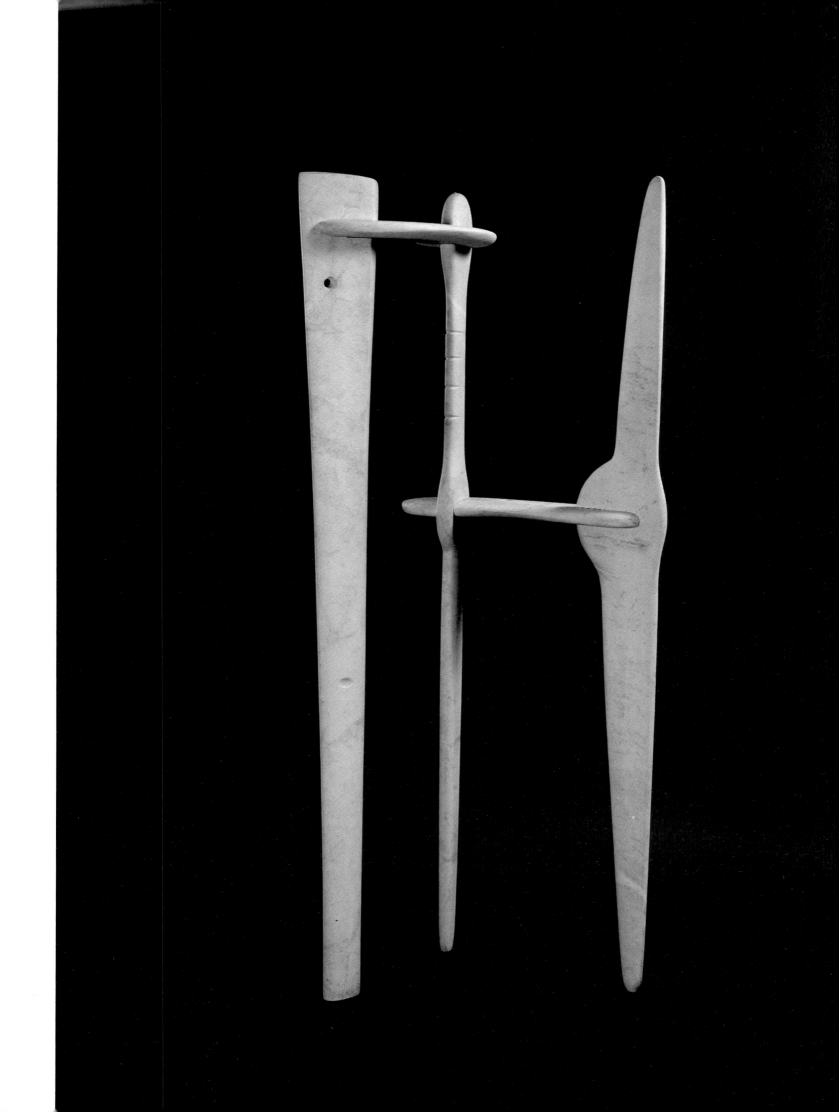

Jorge Eielson. *Red Quipu*. 1964.
Tempera and knotted cloth on canvas. 42¾ × 39⅝ inches (108.6 × 101.7 cm).
NHT.

Right
Richard Lippold. *Bird of Paradise, III*. 1964.
22-karat gold-filled wire. c. 21 × 25 × c. 22 inches
(c. 53.3 × 63.5 × c. 55.9 cm).

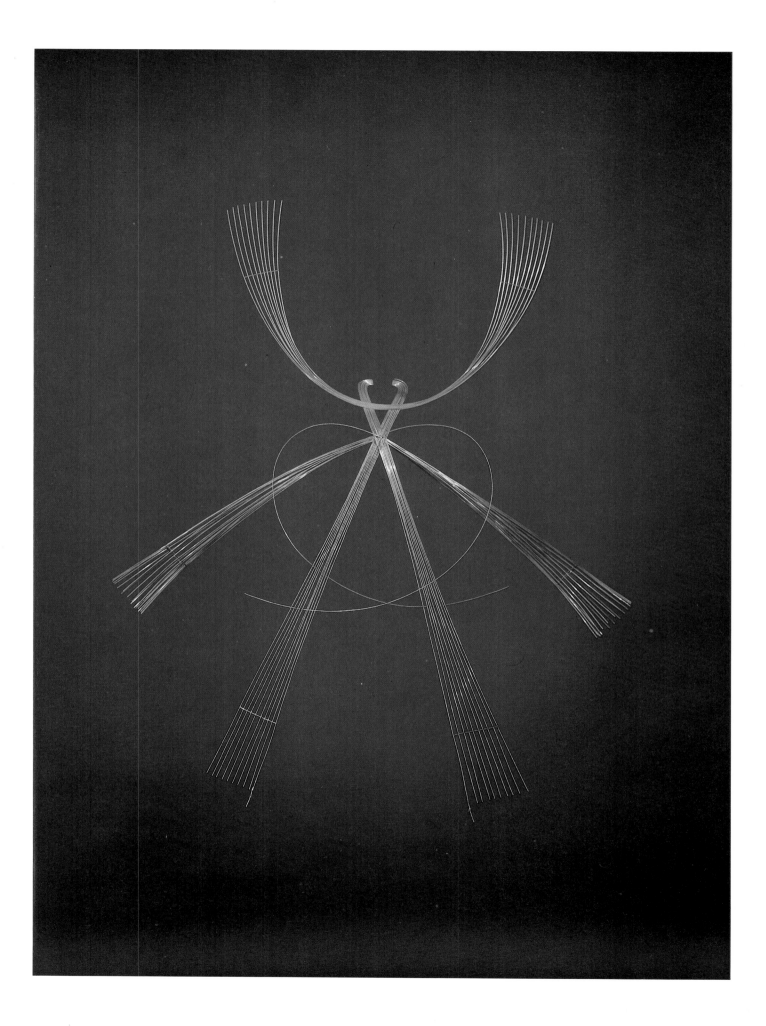

Willem de Kooning. *Mailbox*. 1948.
Oil, enamel, and charcoal on paper. 23 ¼ × 30 inches (59 × 76.2 cm).
Private collection.

Willem de Kooning. *Gansevoort Street*. 1950–51.
Oil on cardboard, mounted on composition board. 30 × 40 inches (76.2 × 101.6 cm).
Collection Mr. and Mrs. Harry W. Anderson.

William Baziotes. *Jungle*. 1951.
Oil on canvas. 50 × 60⅛ inches (127 × 152.7 cm).

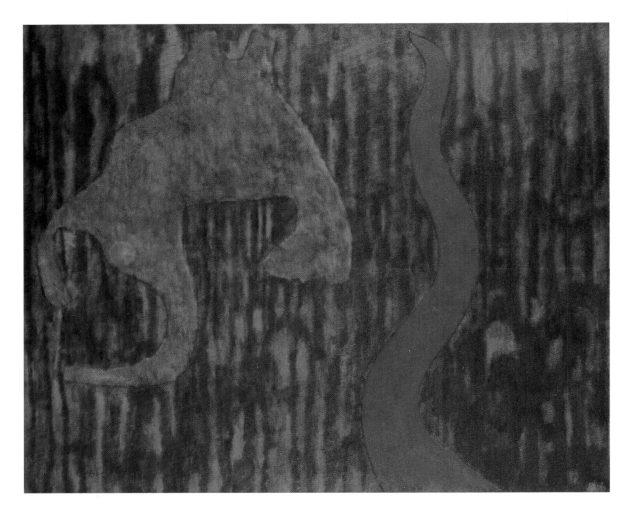

Right
Mark Rothko. *White and Green in Blue*. 1957.
Oil on canvas. 102 × 82 inches (259.1 × 208.3 cm).
Private collection.

174

Robert Motherwell. *Granada: Elegy to the Spanish Republic, II*. 1949.
Oil on paper, mounted on composition board. 48 × 56⅛ inches (121.9 × 142.5 cm).
NHT.

Left
Adolph Gottlieb. *Transfiguration*. 1958.
Oil on canvas. 90 × 60 inches (228.7 × 152.4 cm).
Private collection.

Franz Kline. *Corinthian, II*. 1961.
Oil on canvas. 79¾ × 107 inches (202.6 × 272 cm).
Private collection.

Jackson Pollock. *Number 12, 1952*. 1952.
Oil, duco, and aluminum paint on canvas. 101 ½ × 89 ¼ inches (257.8 × 226.7 cm).
Damaged by fire, 1961; collection The Governor Nelson A. Rockefeller Empire State Plaza.

James Brooks. *Jackson*. 1956.
Oil on canvas. 66¾ × 69¾ inches (169.5 × 177.2 cm).
NHT.

Right
Kenzo Okada. *Kozanji*. 1966.
Oil on canvas. 78½ × 51 inches (199.4 × 129.5 cm).
NHT.

Kengo Okada

Mark Tobey. *Voyagers, III*. 1954.
Tempera on paper. 17¾ × 11⅜ inches (45.1 × 28.8 cm) (sight).

Right
Bradley Walker Tomlin. *Number 5*. 1949.
Oil on canvas. 69⅞ × 37⅞ inches (177.5 × 96.2 cm).
NHT.

Overleaf
Isamu Noguchi. *Black Sun*. 1960–63.
Black Tamba granite. 30 inches (76.2 cm) diameter.
NHT.

Louise Nevelson. *Standing Column from Dawn's Wedding Feast.*1959.
Assemblage: painted wood construction in two sections. 46¼ ×
13½ × 11 inches (117.5 × 34.3 × 28 cm), and 46½ × 14 × 12⅜
inches (118.1 × 35.6 × 31.4 cm).
Private collection.

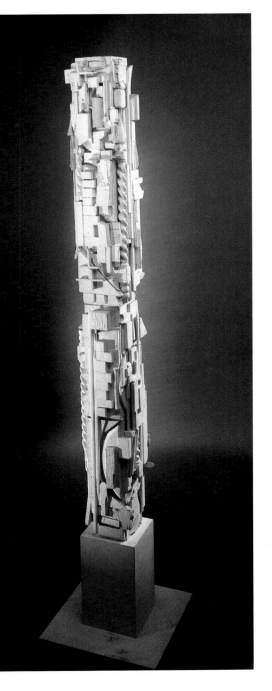

Louise Nevelson. *Transparent Sculpture, VII.* 1967–68.
Plexiglas construction. 20¾ × 10⅞ × 7⅛ inches
(52.7 × 27.6 × 18.1 cm).
NHT.

Louise Nevelson. *Atmosphere and Environment, VI.* 1967.
Enameled aluminum construction. 96 × 102 × 48 inches (243.9 × 259.1 × 121.9 cm).
NHT.

David Smith. *Voltri VI*. 1962.
Steel. 103 × 102¾ × 25½ inches (261.6 × 261 × 64.8 cm).
Collection Mr. and Mrs. Raymond Nasher, Dallas, Texas.

David Smith. *The Banquet*. 1951.
Painted steel. 53 × 80¾ inches (134.6 × 205.1 cm).
NHT.

Jason Seley. *Magister Ludi.* 1962.
Welded chromium-plated steel automobile bumpers.
84 × 45½ × 28 inches (213.4 × 115.6 × 40.5 cm).
NHT.

Right

Herbert Ferber. *Calligraph KC.* 1963–64.
Welded copper. 123 × 68 × 40½ inches (312.6 × 172.7 × 102.9 cm).
NHT.

Ibram Lassaw. *Galaxy of Andromeda*. 1951.
Welded lead over copper. 36⅜ × 39¼ × 20⅝ inches (92.4 × 99.7 × 52.4 cm).
NHT.

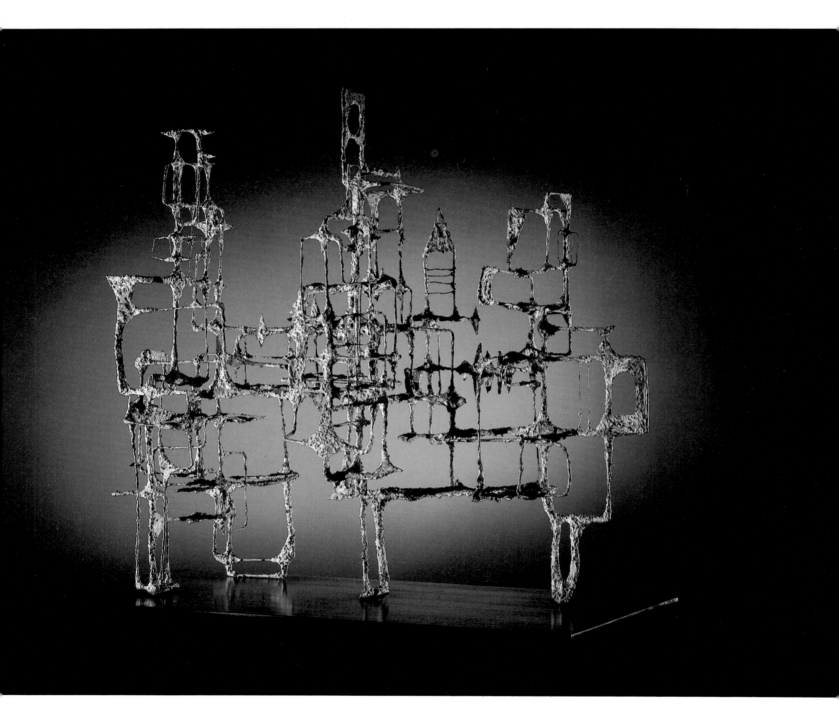

Right
Seymour Lipton. *The Cloak*. 1952.
Welded bronze over steel. 96 inches (244 cm) high.
NHT.

Edgar Negret. *Magical Apparatus, II*. 1954.
Painted iron. 26½ inches (67.3 cm) high.
NHT.

Richard Stankiewicz. *Untitled, XXXII*. 1960.
Welded scrap metal. 37 × 36 × 33 inches (94 × 91.4 × 83.8 cm).
Collection Maurice Vanderwoude, Great Neck, New York.

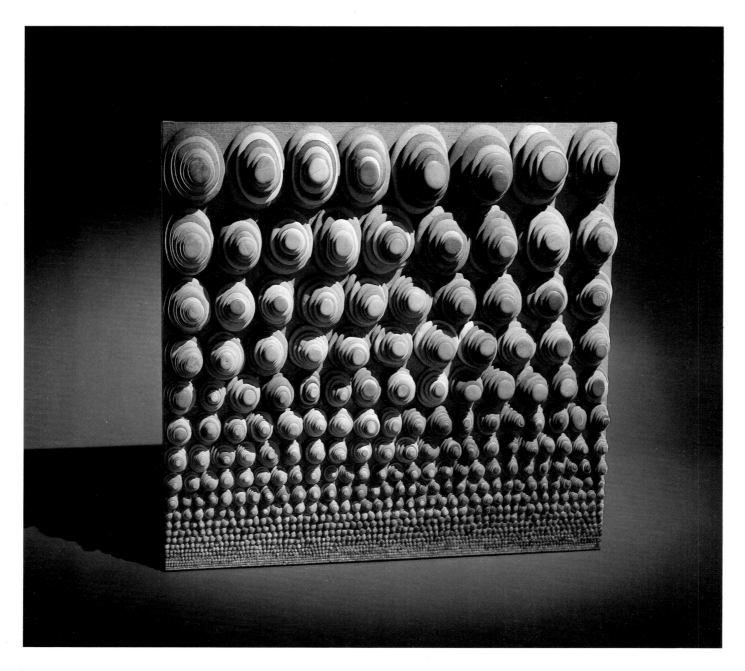

Mary Bauermeister. *High Towered*. 1961–68.
Pebbles on linen-covered wood. 19½ × 19½ × 3⅛ inches (49.5 × 49.5 × 8 cm).
NHT.

Lee Bontecou. Untitled. 1960.
Relief construction of welded metal, canvas, and wire. 55 × 58 × 15 inches (139.7 × 147.3 × 38.1 cm).
NHT.

Raoul Hague. *Annandale-on-Hudson*. 1962–63.
Walnut. 49½ × 32 × 27½ inches (125.7 × 81.3 × 69.9 cm).

Right
Will Horwitt. *Sky*. 1963.
Bronze. 72⅜ inches (183.8 cm) high.
NHT.

Grace Hartigan. *City Life*. 1956.
Oil on canvas. 81 × 98½ inches (205.9 × 250.3 cm).
NHT.

Jasper Johns. *0 Through 9*. 1960.
Oil on canvas. 72 × 54 inches (182.9 × 137.1 cm).
Private collection.

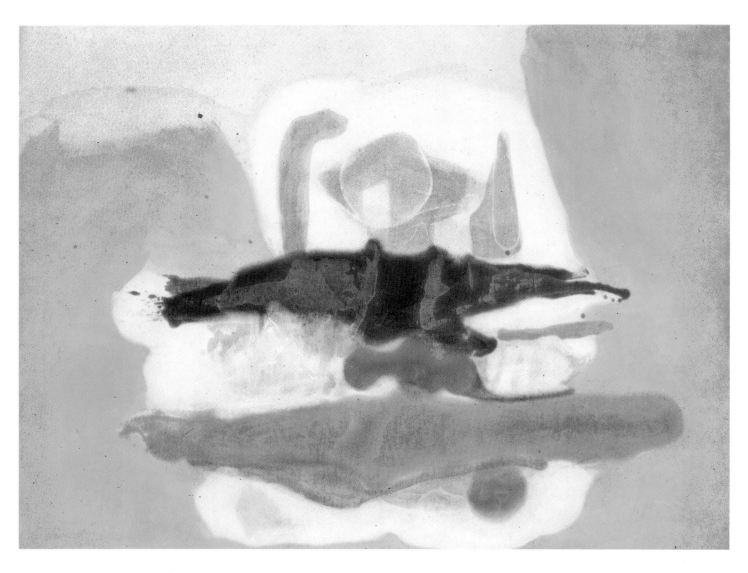

Helen Frankenthaler. *Yellow Clearing.* 1963.
Oil on canvas. 53½ × 69½ (135.9 × 176.5 cm).
Private collection, New York.

Morris Louis. *Floral*. 1959.
Synthetic polymer paint on canvas. 101 × 142 inches (256.7 × 360.9 cm).
Private collection.

Ellsworth Kelly. *Green, Red.* 1965.
Oil on canvas. 90¼ × 90⅜ inches (229.3 × 229.6 cm).
Private collection.

Frank Stella. *Sinjerli Variation, III*. 1968.
Fluorescent synthetic polymer paint on canvas. 122 ½ inches (311.4 cm) diameter.
Collection Sydney and Frances Lewis.

Paul Feeley. *Etamin*. 1965.
Synthetic polymer paint on canvas. 59⅞ × 59⅞ inches (152.1 × 152.1 cm).
Private collection.

Charles B. Hinman. *Number 3.* 1965.
Synthetic polymer paint on shaped canvas over wood framework.
60 × 84 × 16 inches (152.4 × 213.5 × 40.6 cm).
NHT.

Peter Dechar. *Pear 68–11*. 1968.
Oil on canvas. 52 × 72 inches (132.1 × 183 cm).
NHT.

Right
Jean-Paul Riopelle. Untitled. 1954.
Oil on canvas. 51 × 38¼ inches (129.5 × 97.1 cm).
Collection Mr. and Mrs. Andrew Sarlos, Toronto, Ontario.

Andy Warhol. *100 Portraits of Mrs. Nelson A. Rockefeller*. 1968.
Acrylic and silkscreen enamel on canvas. 71¾ × 60 inches (182.2 × 152.4 cm).

Andy Warhol. *Self-Portrait*. 1967.
Acrylic and silkscreen enamel on canvas. 72 × 72 inches (182.9 × 182.9 cm).
Private collection.

George Segal. *Shower Curtain*. 1966.
Plaster. 70 × 50⅝ × 19¾ inches (177.8 × 128.5 × 50.2 cm).
NHT.

George Segal. *Girl Holding Left Arm*. 1973.
Plaster. 30¼ × 28¼ × 7 inches (76.8 × 71.8 × 17.8 cm).
NHT.

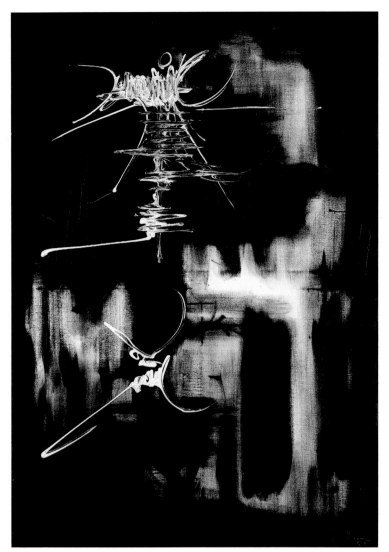

Georges Mathieu. *Painting*. 1955.
Oil on canvas. 34¾ × 57⅜ inches (88.3 × 145.7 cm).

Below

Hans Hartung. *Painting*. 1951.
Oil on canvas. 37¾ × 57⅛ inches (95.9 × 145.1 cm).

Pierre Soulages. *September 10, 1953*. 1953.
Oil on canvas. 76¾ × 51⅛ inches (194.9 × 129.8 cm).
NHT.

Marcos Grigorian. Untitled. 1977.
Dried earth and straw on canvas. 31½ × 31½ × 2½ inches (80 × 80 × 6.3 cm).
Private collection.

Nobuya Abe. *Grey Echo*. 1964.
Encaustic on canvas over wood. 70½ × 70½ inches (179 × 179 cm).
NHT.

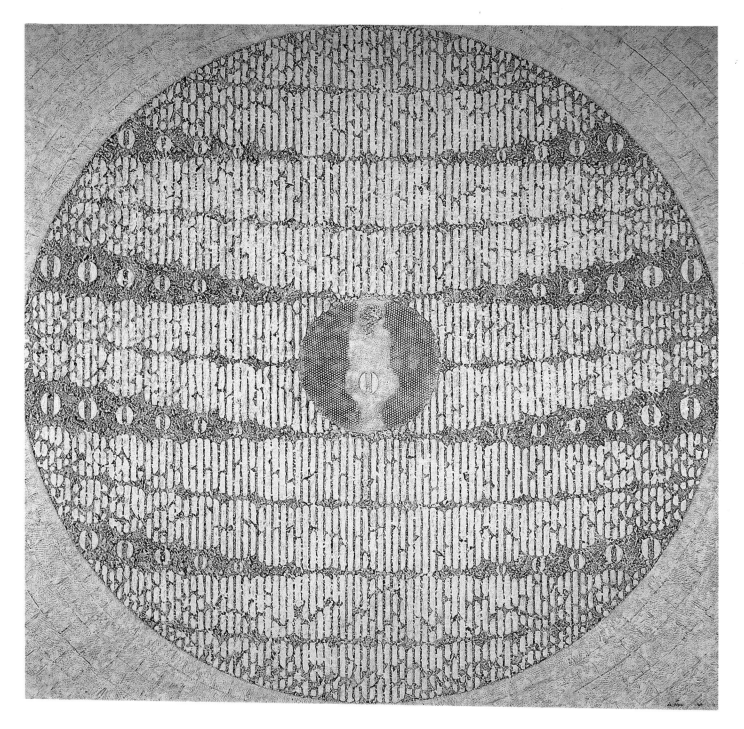

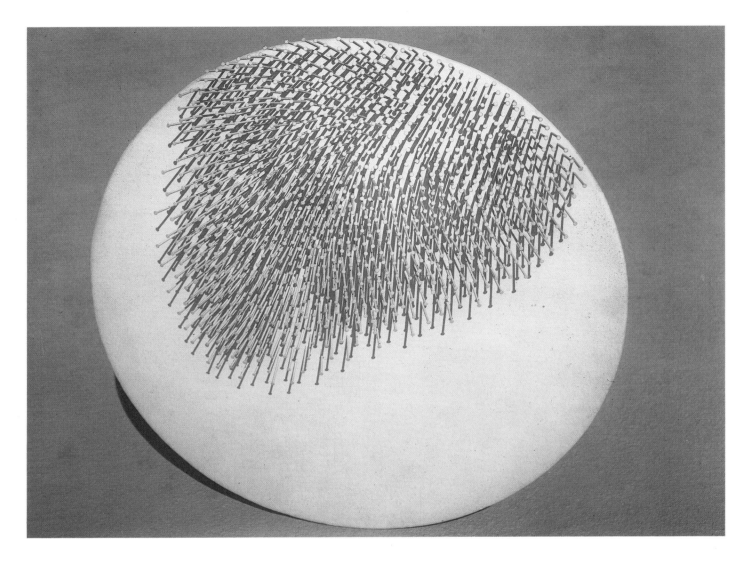

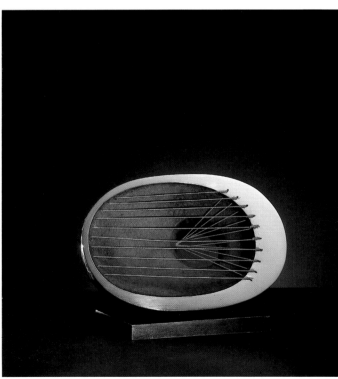

Above
Günther Uecker. *Heart.* 1964.
Nails projecting from canvas-covered board, painted.
34¼ inches (87 cm) diameter.
Collection Frank Sinatra.

Barbara Hepworth. *Hollow Oval.* 1965.
Bronze, with strings, partly painted.
5 × 7⅜ × 3¼ inches (12.7 × 18.8 × 8.2 cm).

Lucio Fontana. *Spatial Concept: Nature I* (right) and
Spatial Concept: Nature II (left). 1968 (after terra cottas of 1959).
Bronze. 34 inches (86.4 cm) and 29½ inches (74.9 cm) diameter, respectively.
NHT.

Masayuki Nagare. *Jubilee*. 1965.
Black granite. 28½ × 11½ × 17½ inches (72.4 × 29.2 × 44.4 cm).
NHT.

Right
Masayuki Nagare. *Bachi*. 1972.
Black granite. 78½ × 33½ × 10⅛ inches (199.4 × 85 × 25.6 cm).

Mirko. *Stele*. 1954.
Cast stone. 113 × 13¾ × 15½ inches (287 × 35 × 39.3 cm).
NHT.

Right
Arnaldo Pomodoro. *Traveler's Column*. 1965–66.
Bronze. 142 inches (460.9 cm) high, 19¾ inches (50.1 cm) diameter.
NHT.

Jean Ipousteguy. *Alexander Before Ecbatane*. 1965.
Bronze. 68 × 144 × 39⅜ inches (172.7 × 366 × 100 cm).
NHT.

Fritz Koenig.*Cross, IV*. 1966.
Bronze. 24 × 5¼ × 3⅝ inches (61 × 13.4 × 9.2 cm).
This sculpture was erected in a quiet glade as a memorial to
Michael C. Rockefeller.
NHT.

George Rickey. *Five Lines in Parallel Planes, II*. 1968.
Stainless steel. 283¾ inches (721 cm) high.
NHT.

Kenneth Snelson. *Fair Leda*. 1968.
Stainless steel tubes and cable. 152½ × 221 × 132½ inches (387.5 × 561.5 × 331.5 cm).
NHT.

Jean Dubuffet. *Landscape with Butterflies (Paysage aux colias)*. 1957.
Butterfly wings, gouache, and paper. 14½ × 9½ inches (37 × 24 cm).

Below
Jiří Kolář. *Battle*. 1968.
Pasted papers. 10¾ × 18 inches (27.3 × 45.7 cm).
Private collection.

Right
Jean Dubuffet. *L'Erection logologique bleue*. 1967–69.
Enameled concrete. 132 × 97½ × 37½ inches (335.5 × 247.8 × 95.2 cm).
NHT.

Takis. *Signal*. 1955–58.
Metal rods, etc. 33¾ × c. 36 × c. 12 inches (85.7 × c. 91.5 × c. 30.5 cm).

Left
Benni Efrat. *Barbara (Hommage to Barbara Reise)*. 1971–72.
Five square slabs of stone in a row, grooved to contain a cable
across the stones. 8 × 141¾ × 33½ inches (20.3 × 306.3 × 85.1 cm).
NHT.

Pol Bury. *Twenty-nine Balls on Two Slanting Planes*. 1967.
Motor-driven copper construction. 14⅛ × 13⅞ × 12 inches
(35.9 × 35.2 × 30.5 cm).
Collection Dr. and Mrs. Frederick R. Mebel.

Right
Horst Egon Kalinowski. *The Eye of Horus*. 1964.
Assemblage: leather over wood construction. 30 × 21⅞ × 9 inches
(76.2 × 55.6 × 22.9 cm).
Collection Mr. and Mrs. Thomas B. Morgan.

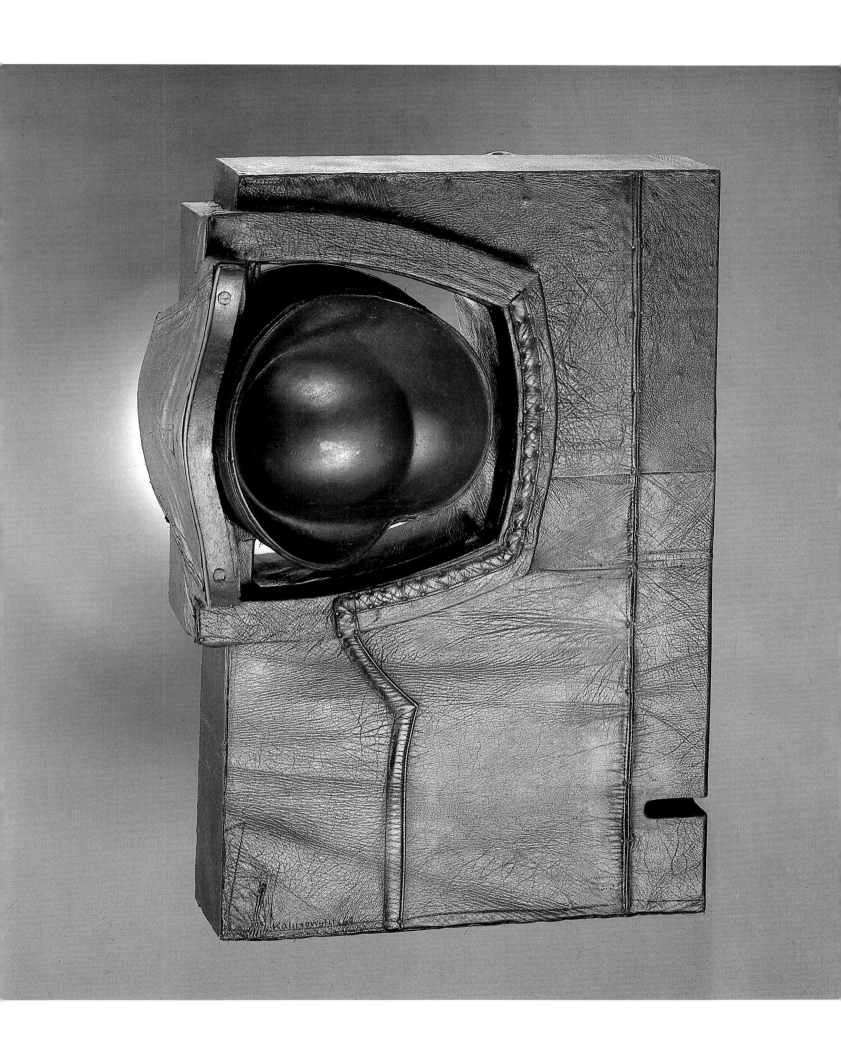

James Rosati. *Lippincott II*. 1965–69.
Cor-ten steel, painted. 106 × 189 × 48 inches (269.2 × 480.4 × 122 cm).
NHT.

Eduardo Paolozzi. *Akapotic Rose*. 1965.
Cast and welded aluminum. 74¾ × 111 × 50 inches (189.2 × 281.9 × 127 cm).
NHT.

234

Left
Gio Pomodoro. *The Great Ghibellini Lady.* 1965.
Marble. 78 × 80 × 29 inches (198 × 203.2 × 73.5 cm).
NHT.

Gottfried Honegger. *Volume 11.* 1969.
Polyester cast. 33⅛ × 33 × 13⅜ inches (84.1 × 83.8 × 34 cm).
NHT.

Left
Max Bill. *Triangular Surface in Space*. 1962.
Rose granite on gray granite column. 78¾ × 35½ inches (200 × 90.2 cm).
NHT.

Fritz Wotruba. *Figure*. 1961–62.
Marble. 70½ × 13 × 18¼ inches (179 × 33 × 46.3 cm).
NHT.

Overleaf
Clement Meadmore. *Double Up*. 1975.
Cor-ten steel. 240 × 186 × 150 inches
(610 × 472.7 × 381.2 cm). NHT.

Clement Meadmore. U Turn. 1968.
Cor-ten steel, painted. 87 × 168 × 132 inches (221 × 427 × 335.5 cm).
NHT.

Tony Smith. *Cigarette*. 1961.
Painted steel. 181 × 306 × 223 inches (459 × 777 × 566 cm).
NHT.

Marino Marini. *Horse*. 1951.
Bronze. 84 inches (213.5 cm) high.
NHT.

Right
James Buchman. *Podium*. 1974.
Granite and steel. 85 × 100 × 74 inches (216 × 254 × 188 cm).
NHT.

Richard Fleischner. *Maze*. 1972.
Tufa. 56 × 114 × 204 inches (142 × 288 × 418.5 cm).
NHT.

BIBLIOGRAPHY

GENERAL WORKS ON MODERN ART

Arnason, H. H. *History of Modern Art: Painting, Sculpture, Architecture.* Englewood Cliffs, N. J.: Prentice-Hall, 1977.

Barr, Alfred H., Jr. *Cubism and Abstract Art.* New York: The Museum of Modern Art, 1936; reissued 1974.

———, ed. *Masters of Modern Art.* New York: The Museum of Modern Art, 1954.

Cahill, Holger. *New Horizons in American Art.* New York: The Museum of Modern Art, 1936.

Geldzahler, Henry. *American Painting in the 20th Century.* New York: The Metropolitan Museum of Art, 1965.

Goodrich, Lloyd, and Baur, John I. H. *American Art of Our Century.* New York: Praeger, 1961.

Greenberg, Clement. *Art and Culture: Critical Essays.* Boston: Beacon Press, 1965.

Haftmann, Werner. *Painting in the Twentieth Century.* 2 vols. New York: Praeger, 1965.

Hamilton, George Heard. *Nineteenth and Twentieth Century Art.* New York: Harry N. Abrams, 1970.

Hunter, Sam. *Modern American Painting and Sculpture.* New York: Dell, 1959.

———. *American Art of the Twentieth Century,* New York: Harry N. Abrams, 1972.

Hunter, Sam, and Jacobus, John. *Modern Art from Post-Impressionism to the Present.* New York: Harry N. Abrams, 1976.

Johnson, Ellen H. *Modern Art and the Object: A Century of Changing Attitudes.* New York: Harper & Row, 1977.

Kozloff, Max. *Renderings: Critical Essays on a Century of Modern Art.* New York: Simon and Schuster, 1968.

Kramer, Hilton. *The Age of the Avant-Garde: An Art Chronicle of 1956–1972.* New York: Farrar, Straus and Giroux, 1973.

Lucie-Smith, Edward. *Late Modern: The Visual Arts Since 1945.* New York: Praeger, 1969.

Read, Sir Herbert Edward. *The Philosophy of Modern Art.* Greenwich, Conn.: Fawcett, 1967.

Ritchie, Andrew Carnduff. *Abstract Painting and Sculpture in America.* New York: The Museum of Modern Art, 1951.

Rose, Barbara. *American Art Since 1900: A Critical History.* New York: Praeger, 1967.

———. *American Painting: The Twentieth-Century.* Geneva: Skira, 1970.

Rosenblum, Robert. *Cubism and Twentieth-Century Art.* New York: Harry N. Abrams, 1961.

Russell, John. *The Meanings of Modern Art.* New York: The Museum of Modern Art and Harper & Row, 1981.

Sandler, Irving. *The Triumph of American Painting: A History of Abstract Expressionism.* New York: Praeger, 1970.

Schapiro, Meyer. *Modern Art: 19th and 20th Centuries.* New York: George Braziller, 1978.

Steinberg, Leo. *Other Criteria: Confrontations with Twentieth-Century Art.* New York and London: Oxford University Press, 1972.

Sylvester, David. *Modern Art from Fauvism to Abstract Expressionism.* New York: Watts, 1966.

WORKS ON THE NELSON A. ROCKEFELLER COLLECTION

"Capitalizing on a Collection." *Time,* November 13, 1978.

Carter, Malcolm. "Nelson Rockefeller: I Know Exactly What I Like." *Artnews,* May 1978.

Donovan, Robert J. "Rockefeller Exhibits a Collector's Art and Artistry." *The Los Angeles Times,* November 28, 1971.

Dudar, Helen. "Nelson Now." *New York Magazine,* September 25, 1978.

Goldwater, Robert. "New York, Governor Nelson A. Rockefeller: Primitive Art and the Twentieth-Century." In *Great Private Collections.* Edited by Douglas Cooper, Introduction by Kenneth Clark. New York: Macmillan, 1963.

Goodman, Cynthia. *From the Collection of Governor Nelson A. Rockefeller.* Albany, N.Y., 1981.

Keller, Dominik. "Nelson Aldrich Rockefeller," with essays by Henry A. Kissinger, Samuel E. Bleecker, William S. Lieberman, and Douglas Newton. *Du: Die Kunstzeitschrift* (Zürich), May 1979.

Lieberman, William S. *Twentieth-Century Art from the Nelson Aldrich Rockefeller Collection.* New York: The Museum of Modern Art, 1969.

Loercher, Diana. "A Matter of Taste." *Christian Science Monitor,* May 1978.

Loring, John, and Spector, Stephen. "Vice Presidential Mansion: The Nelson Rockefellers' Residence in Washington, D.C." *Architectural Digest,* March/April 1976.

New York, Herbert H. Lehman College, The City University of New York. *Picasso Tapestries from the Collection of Nelson A. Rockefeller.* 1971.

New York, New School Art Center. *Governor Rockefeller's Collection from the Albany Mansion.* 1967.

Partington, Susan Trowbridge. "Tarrytown: The Nelson A. Rockefeller Collection at Pocantico Hills." *Of Westchester,* vol. 3, no. 2, March/April 1971.

du Plessix, Francine. "Anatomy of a Collector: Nelson A. Rockefeller." *Art in America,* no. 2, 1965.

Rockefeller, Nelson A. "The Governor Lectures on Art." *The New York Times Magazine,* April 9, 1967.

———. "Reflections on Art and Politics." *Famous Artists Magazine,* vol. 16, no. 1, Autumn 1967.

Saarinen, Aline B. *The Proud Possessors: The Lives, Times and Tastes of Some Adventurous American Art Collectors.* New York: Random House, 1958.

Solomon, Stephen. "Nelson Rockefeller Turns His Passion for Art into a Business." *Fortune,* October 23, 1978.

Stevens, Mark. "Rocky's Art Clones." *Newsweek,* October 16, 1978.

Truex, Van Day. "Jean-Michel Frank Remembered." *Architectural Digest,* September/October 1976.

SELECTED WORKS ON ARTISTS IN THE NELSON A. ROCKEFELLER COLLECTION

Abe, Nobuya

New York, The Museum of Modern Art. *The New Japanese Painting and Sculpture.* 1966.

Appel, Karel

Toronto, Rothmans of Pall Mall Canada, Ltd. *Appel's Appels.* 1972.

Archipenko, Alexander

Karshan, Donald H. *Archipenko: International Visionary.* Washington, D.C.: Smithsonian Institution Press, 1969.

Armitage, Kenneth

Penrose, Roland. *Kenneth Armitage.* Amviswil: Bodensee-Verlag, 1960.

Arp, Jean

Arp, Hans [Jean]. *On My Way: Poetry and Essays, 1912–1947.* New York: Wittenborn, Schultz, 1948.

Giedion-Welcker, Carola. *Jean Arp.* New York: Harry N. Abrams, 1957.

Last, R. W. *Hans Arp: The Poet of Dadaism.* London: Wolff, 1969.

Read, Sir Herbert Edward. *The Art of Jean Arp.* New York: Harry N. Abrams, 1968.

Barlach, Ernst

Carls, Carl Dietrich. *Ernst Barlach*. New York: Praeger, 1969.

Baziotes, William

New York, The Solomon R. Guggenheim Museum. *William Baziotes: A Memorial Exhibition*. 1965. Introduction by Lawrence Alloway.

Beckmann, Max

Selz, Peter. *Max Beckmann*. New York: The Museum of Modern Art, 1964.

Boccioni, Umberto

Kozloff, Max. *Cubism/Futurism*. New York: Charterhouse, 1973.

Soby, James Thrall, and Barr, Alfred H., Jr. *Twentieth-Century Italian Art*. New York: The Museum of Modern Art, 1949.

Taylor, Joshua C. *Futurism*. New York: The Museum of Modern Art, 1961.

Bontecou, Lee

New York, Whitney Museum of American Art. *Annual Exhibition of Sculpture and Drawings*. 1960.

Brancusi, Constantin

Geist, Sidney. *Brancusi: A Study of the Sculpture*. New York: Grossman, 1968.

Giedion-Welcker, Carola. *Constantin Brancusi*. New York: George Braziller, 1959.

Zervos, Christian, ed. *Constantin Brancusi: Sculpture, Peintures, Fresques, Dessins*. Paris: Cahiers d'Art, 1957.

Braque, Georges

Cogniat, Raymond. *Braque*. New York: Crown, 1970.

Cooper, Douglas. *Braque: The Great Years*. Chicago: The Art Institute of Chicago, 1972.

Hope, Henry R. *Georges Braque*. New York: The Museum of Modern Art, 1949.

Leymarie, Jean. *Braque*. Geneva: Skira, 1961.

Richardson, John, ed. *G. Braque*. Greenwich, Conn.: New York Graphic Society, 1961.

Russell, John. *Georges Braque*. Garden City, N.Y.: Phaidon, 1951.

Brooks, James

Hunter, Sam. *James Brooks*. New York: Whitney Museum of American Art, 1963.

Butler, Reg

Butler, Reg. *Creative Development*. New York: Horizon Press, 1963.

Calder, Alexander

Arnason, H. H., and Guerrero, Pedro. *Alexander Calder*. New York: Van Nostrand, 1966.

London, The Tate Gallery. *Alexander Calder: Sculpture, Mobiles*. 1962.

New York, The Solomon R. Guggenheim Museum. *Alexander Calder: A Retrospective Exhibition*. 1964.

Rose, Bernice. *A Salute to Alexander Calder*. New York: The Museum of Modern Art, 1969.

Sweeney, James Johnson. *Alexander Calder*. 2d. ed., rev. New York: The Museum of Modern Art, 1951.

Castellanos, Julio

Chicago, The Art Institute of Chicago. *The U.S. Collects Pan-American Art*. 1959.

Chadwick, Lynn

Read, Sir Herbert Edward. *Lynn Chadwick*. Amviswil: Bodensee-Verlag, 1960.

Chagall, Marc

Cassou, Jean. *Chagall*. New York: Praeger, 1965.

Meyer, Franz. *Marc Chagall*. New York: Harry N. Abrams, 1964.

de Chirico, Giorgio

Soby, James Thrall. *Giorgio de Chirico*. New York: The Museum of Modern Art, 1955.

Delvaux, Paul

Nadeau, Maurice. *Les Dessins de Paul Delvaux*. Paris: Denoël, 1967.

Demuth, Charles

Farnham, Emily. *Charles Demuth: His Life, Psychology, and Works*. Ann Arbor: University Microfilms International, 1979.

van Dongen, Kees

New York, Leonard Hutton Galleries. *Van Dongen: A Comprehensive Exhibition of Paintings, 1900 to 1925*. 1965.

Dubuffet, Jean

New York, The Solomon R. Guggenheim Museum. *Jean Dubuffet: A Retrospective*. 1973.

Selz, Peter. *The Work of Jean Dubuffet*. New York: The Museum of Modern Art, 1962.

Duchamp-Villon, Raymond

Agee, William C. *Raymond Duchamp-Villon, 1876 to 1918*. With an Introduction by George Heard Hamilton. New York: Walker, 1968.

New York, The Solomon R. Guggenheim Museum. *Jacques Villon, Raymond Duchamp-Villon and Marcel Duchamp*. 1957.

Paris, Galerie Louis Carré. *Duchamp-Villon: Le Cheval Majeur*. 1966.

Eielson, Jorge

New York, Center for Inter-American Relations. *Looking South: Latin American Art in New York Collections*. 1972.

Ernst, Max

Lieberman, William S., ed. *Max Ernst*. New York: The Museum of Modern Art, 1961.

New York, The Solomon R. Guggenheim Museum. *Max Ernst: A Retrospective*. 1975.

Feeley, Paul

New York, The Solomon R. Guggenheim Museum. *Paul Feeley, 1910 to 1966: A Memorial Exhibition*. 1968.

Feininger, Lyonel

Ness, June L. *Lyonel Feininger*. New York: Praeger, 1974.

Ferber, Herbert

Anderson, Wayne V. *The Sculpture of Herbert Ferber*. Minneapolis, Minn.: Walker Art Center, 1962.

Fleischner, Richard

Amherst, Mass., University of Massachusetts, University Gallery. *Richard Fleischner*. 1977.

Fontana, Lucio

New York, The Solomon R. Guggenheim Museum. *Lucio Fontana, 1899–1968: A Retrospective*. 1977.

Frankenthaler, Helen

Rose, Barbara. *Helen Frankenthaler*. New York: Harry N. Abrams, 1972.

Gabo, Naum

Newman, Teresa. *Naum Gabo, The Constructive Process*. London: The Tate Gallery, 1976.

New York, The Museum of Modern Art. *Naum Gabo and Antoine Pevsner*. 1948.

Giacometti, Alberto

Hohl, Reinhold. *Alberto Giacometti*. New York: Harry N. Abrams, 1972.

New York, The Solomon R. Guggenheim Museum. *Alberto Giacometti*. 1974.

Selz, Peter. *Alberto Giacometti*. New York: The Museum of Modern Art, 1965.

Glarner, Fritz

Edgar, Natalie. *Fritz Glarner*. San Francisco: San Francisco Museum of Art, 1970.

Miller, Dorothy C., ed. *Twelve Americans*. New York: The Museum of Modern Art, 1956.

Gleizes, Albert

Robbins, Daniel. *Albert Gleizes, 1881–1953: A Retrospective Exhibition*. New York: The Solomon R. Guggenheim Museum, 1964.

Gonzalez, Julio

New York, The Museum of Modern Art. *Julio Gonzalez: Retrospective Exhibition*. 1964.

Withers, Josephine. *Julio Gonzalez: Sculpture in Iron*. New York: New York University Press, 1977.

Gorky, Arshile

Levy, Julien. *Arshile Gorky*. New York: Harry N. Abrams, 1966.

Rosenberg, Harold. *Arshile Gorky: The Man, the Time, the Idea*. New York: Horizon Press, 1962.

Schwabacher, Ethel K. *Arshile Gorky*. New York: Whitney Museum of American Art, 1957.

Seitz, William C. *Arshile Gorky: Paintings, Drawings, Studies*. New York: The Museum of Modern Art, 1962.

Gottlieb, Adolph

Doty, Robert, and Waldman, Diane. *Adolph Gottlieb*. New York: Praeger, 1968.

Gris, Juan

Kahnweiler, Daniel-Henry. *Juan Gris: His Life and Work*. New York: Harry N. Abrams, 1969.

Soby, James Thrall. *Juan Gris*. New York: The Museum of Modern Art, 1958.

Hartigan, Grace

Friedman, B. H., ed. *School of New York: Some Younger American Artists*. New York: Grove Press, 1960.

Miller, Dorothy C., ed. *Twelve Americans*. New York: The Museum of Modern Art, 1956.

Hartung, Hans

Apollonio, Umbro. *Hans Hartung*. New York: Harry N. Abrams, 1972.

Hepworth, Barbara

Bowness, Alan, ed. *The Sculpture of Barbara Hepworth, 1960 to 1969*. New York: Praeger, 1971.

Hodin, Josef Paul. *Barbara Hepworth*. London: Lund, Humphries, 1961.

Read, Sir Herbert Edward. *Barbara Hepworth Carvings and Drawings*. London: Lund, Humphries, 1952.

Honegger, Gottfried

Forster, Kurt W. *Gottfried Honegger: Work from 1939 to 1971*. Teufen, Switzerland: Arthur Niggli, 1972.

Ipousteguy, Jean

Paris, Fondation Nationale des Arts Graphiques et Plastiques. *Ipousteguy: Sculptures et dessins de 1957 à 1978*. 1978.

Jawlensky, Alexey

Baltimore, The Baltimore Museum of Art. *Alexej Jawlensky*. 1965.

New York, Leonard Hutton Galleries. *Alexej Jawlensky*. 1965.

Johns, Jasper

Crichton, Michael. *Jasper Johns*. New York: Harry N. Abrams, 1977.

Steinberg, Leo. *Jasper Johns*. New York: Wittenborn, Schultz, 1963.

Kalinowski, Horst Egon

Vandrey, Max. *Kalinowski*. Hannover: Kestner-Gesellschaft, 1969.

Kandinsky, Wassily

Bill, Max, ed. *Wassily Kandinsky*. Boston: Institute of Contemporary Art (in association with Maeght, Paris), 1951.

Grohmann, Will. *Wassily Kandinsky: Life and Work*. New York: Harry N. Abrams, 1958.

Roethel, Hans K., with Benjamin, Jean K. *Kandinsky*. New York: Hudson Hills Press, 1979.

Kelly, Ellsworth

Coplans, John. *Ellsworth Kelly*. New York: Harry N. Abrams, 1972.

Goossen, E. C. *Ellsworth Kelly*. New York: The Museum of Modern Art, 1973.

Kiesler, Frederick J.

Lipman, Jean, and Franc, Helen M. *Bright Stars: American Painting and Sculpture Since 1776*. New York: E. P. Dutton, 1976.

Miller, Dorothy C., ed. *Fifteen Americans*. New York: The Museum of Modern Art, 1952.

Klee, Paul

Grohmann, Will. *Paul Klee*. New York: Harry N. Abrams, 1954.

Haftmann, Werner. *The Mind and Work of Paul Klee*. New York: Praeger, 1954.

New York, The Solomon R. Guggenheim Museum. *Paul Klee, 1879 to 1940: A Retrospective Exhibition*. 1967.

Kline, Franz

Gordon, John. *Franz Kline: 1910 to 1962*. New York: Whitney Museum of American Art, 1968.

Washington, D.C., Gallery of Modern Art. *Franz Kline Memorial Exhibition*. 1962.

Kolář, Jiří

New York, The Solomon R. Guggenheim Museum. *Jiří Kolář*. 1975.

Kolbe, Georg

Pinder, Wilhelm. *Georg Kolbe*. Berlin: Rembrandt, 1937.

de Kooning, Willem

Hess, Thomas B. *Willem de Kooning*. New York: The Museum of Modern Art, 1968.

Rosenberg, Harold. *De Kooning*. New York: Harry N. Abrams, 1974.

Waldman, Diane. *Willem de Kooning in East Hampton*. New York: The Solomon R. Guggenheim Museum, 1978.

Lachaise, Gaston

Los Angeles, Los Angeles County Museum of Art, and New York, Whitney Museum of American Art. *Gaston Lachaise Sculpture and Drawings*. 1964.

Nordland, Gerald. *Lachaise: The Man and His Work*. New York: George Braziller, 1974.

Lam, Wifredo

Fouchet, Max-Pol. *Wifredo Lam*. Barcelona: Ediciones Polígrafa, 1976.

Lassaw, Ibram

Goossen, E. C., Goldwater, R., and Sandler, I. *Three American Sculptors*. New York: Grove Press, 1959.

Léger, Fernand

Delevoy, Robert L. *Léger: Biographical and Critical Study*. Geneva: Skira, 1962.

Green, Christopher. *Léger and the Avant-Garde*. New Haven: Yale University Press, 1976.

Tériade, E. *Fernand Léger*. Paris: Cahiers d'Art, 1928.

Zervos, Christian. *Fernand Léger: Oeuvres de 1905 à 1952*. Paris: Cahiers d'Art, 1952.

Lehmbruck, Wilhelm

Heller, Reinhold. *The Art of Wilhelm Lehmbruck*. Washington, D.C.: National Gallery of Art, 1972.

Hoff, August. *Wilhelm Lehmbruck: Life and Work*. New York: Praeger, 1969.

Liberman, Alexander

Goossen, E. C. "Alex Liberman: American Sculptor." *Art International*, vol. 15, October 1971.

Lipchitz, Jacques

Goldwater, Robert. *Jacques Lipchitz*. New York: Universe, 1959.

Hammacher, A. M. *Jacques Lipchitz*. New York: Harry N. Abrams, 1975.

Hope, Henry R. *The Sculpture of Jacques Lipchitz*. New York: The Museum of Modern Art, 1954.

Lippold, Richard

Bernier, Rosamond. "Richard Lippold." *L'Oeil* (Paris), no. 64, April 1960.

Lipton, Seymour

Elsen, Albert. *Seymour Lipton*. New York: Harry N. Abrams, 1972.

Louis, Morris

Freid, Michael. *Morris Louis*. New York: Harry N. Abrams, 1971.

New York: The Solomon R. Guggenheim Museum. *Morris Louis, 1912 to 1962: Memorial Exhibition, Paintings from 1954 to 1960*. 1963.

Maillol, Aristide

Chevalier, Denys. *Maillol*. New York: Crown, 1970.

New York, The Solomon R. Guggenheim Museum. *Aristide Maillol: 1861 to 1944*. 1975.

Waldemar, George. *Aristide Maillol*. Greenwich, Conn.: New York Graphic Society, 1965.

Marcks, Gerhard

Los Angeles, University Art Galleries. *Gerhard Marcks*. 1969.

Marini, Marino

Hammacher, A. M. *Marino Marini: Sculpture, Paintings, Drawings*. New York: Harry N. Abrams, 1971.

Marquet, Albert

Jourdain, Francis. *Marquet*. Paris: Cercle d' Art, 1959.

Mastroianni, Umberto

Ponente, Nello. *Mastroianni*. Rome: Edizioni d'Arte Moderne, 1963.

Mathieu, Georges

Quignon-Fleuret, Dominique. *Mathieu*. New York: Crown, 1963.

Matisse, Henri

Barr, Alfred H., Jr. *Matisse: His Art and His Public*. New York: The Museum of Modern Art, 1951.

Cowart, Jack. *Henri Matisse: Paper Cut-outs*. St. Louis: The Saint Louis Art Museum, 1977.

Elderfield, John. *Matisse in The Collection of The Museum of Modern Art*. New York: The Museum of Modern Art, 1978.

———. *Henri Matisse Cut-outs*. New York: George Braziller, 1979.

Elsen, Albert. *The Sculpture of Henri Matisse*. New York: Harry N. Abrams, 1972.

Gowing, Lawrence. *Matisse*. London: Arts Council of Great Britain and Hayward Gallery, 1968.

Legg, Alicia. *The Sculpture of Matisse*. New York: The Museum of Modern Art, 1972.

Leymarie, Jean, Read, Herbert, and Lieberman, William S. *Henri Matisse*. Berkeley: University of California Press, 1966.

Paris, Musée National d'Art Moderne. *Henri Matisse: Dessins et Sculpture*. 1975.

Philadelphia: The Philadelphia Museum of Art. *Henri Matisse: Retrospective Exhibition of Paintings, Drawings, and Sculpture Organized in Collaboration with the Artist*. 1948.

Wheeler, Monroe. *The Last Works of Henri Matisse: Large Cut Gouaches*. New York: The Museum of Modern Art, 1961.

Miró, Joan

Diehl, Gaston. *Miró*. New York: Crown, 1974.

Dupin, Jacques. *Miró*. New York: Harry N. Abrams, 1961.

Penrose, Sir Roland. *Miró*. New York: Harry N. Abrams, 1970.

Rubin, William. *Miró in The Collection of The Museum of Modern Art*. New York: The Museum of Modern Art, 1973.

Soby, James Thrall. *Miró*. New York: The Museum of Modern Art, 1959.

Sweeney, James Johnson. *Joan Miró*. New York: The Museum of Modern Art, 1941.

Modigliani, Amedeo

Fifield, William. *Modigliani*. New York: Morrow, 1976.

Lieberman, William S. *The Nudes of Modigliani*. New York: Perls Galleries, 1966.

Soby, James Thrall. *Modigliani: Paintings, Drawings, Sculpture*. 3d ed., rev. New York: The Museum of Modern Art, 1963.

Mondrian, Piet

Hunter, Sam. *Mondrian: 1872 to 1944*. New York: Harry N. Abrams, 1958.

New York, The Solomon R. Guggenheim Museum. *Piet Mondrian, 1872 to 1944: Centennial Exhibition*. 1971.

Moore, Henry

Finn, David. *A Henry Moore Odyssey: His Sculptures in Their Environments*. Foreword by Kenneth Clark, Commentaries by Henry Moore. New York: Harry N. Abrams, 1976.

Melville, Robert. *Henry Moore: Sculpture and Drawings, 1921 to 1969*. New York: Harry N. Abrams, 1970.

Read, Herbert. *Henry Moore: A Study of His Life and Work*. New York: Praeger, 1965.

Russell, John. *Henry Moore*. New York: Putnam, 1968.

Seldis, Henry J. *Henry Moore in America*. Los Angeles: Los Angeles County Museum of Art, 1973.

Sylvester, David. *Henry Moore*. New York: Praeger, 1968.

Morandi, Giorgio

Guiffre, Guido. *Morandi*. London and New York: Hamlyn, 1971.

Motherwell, Robert

Arnason, H. H. *Robert Motherwell*. New York: Harry N. Abrams, 1977.

O'Hara, Frank. *Robert Motherwell*. New York: The Museum of Modern Art, 1965.

Münter, Gabriele

New York, Leonard Hutton Galleries. *Gabriele Münter: Fifty Years of Her Art*. 1966.

Nadelman, Elie

Kirstein, Lincoln. *Elie Nadelman*. New York: The Eakins Press, 1973.

New York, Whitney Museum of American Art. *The Sculpture and Drawings of Elie Nadelman: 1882 to 1946*. 1975.

Nevelson, Louise

Friedman, Martin. *Nevelson: Wood Sculptures*, New York: E. P. Dutton, 1973.

Glimcher, Arnold. *Louise Nevelson*. New York: E. P. Dutton, 1976.

Gordon, John. *Louise Nevelson Retrospective Exhibition*. New York: Whitney Museum of American Art, 1967.

Noguchi, Isamu

Gordon, John. *Isamu Noguchi*. New York: Whitney Museum of American Art, 1968.

Hunter, Sam. *Isamu Noguchi*. New York: Abbeville Press, 1978.

Paolozzi, Eduardo

London, Arts Council of Great Britain. *Eduardo Paolozzi: Sculpture, Drawings, Collages and Graphics*. 1976.

Pascin, Jules

Diehl, Gaston. *Pascin*. New York: Crown, 1968.

Werner, Alfred. *Pascin*. New York: Harry N. Abrams, 1962.

Picasso, Pablo

Barr, Alfred H., Jr. *Picasso, Fifty Years of His Art*. 3d. ed. New York: The Museum of Modern Art, 1955; reissued 1974.

———, ed. *Picasso: 75th Anniversary Exhibition*. New York: The Museum of Modern Art, 1957.

Boeck, Wilhelm, and Sabartes, Jaime. *Picasso*. New York: Harry N. Abrams, 1955.

Daix, Pierre. *Picasso*. New York: Praeger, 1964.

Picasso (continued)

Leymarie, Jean. *Picasso: The Artist of the Century*. Geneva: Skira and New York: Rizzoli, 1976.

O'Brien, Patrick. *Pablo Ruiz Picasso: A Biography*. New York: Putnam, 1976.

Penrose, Roland. *Portrait of Picasso*. London: Lund, Humphries, 1956; rev. ed. 1972.

———. *The Sculpture of Picasso*. Chronology by Alicia Legg. New York: The Museum of Modern Art, 1967.

———. *Picasso: His Life and Work*. New York: Harper & Row, 1973.

Rubin, William. *Picasso in the Collection of The Museum of Modern Art*. New York: The Museum of Modern Art, 1972.

———, ed. *Pablo Picasso: A Retrospective*. Chronology by Jane Fluegel. New York: The Museum of Modern Art, 1980.

Zervos, Christian. *Pablo Picasso*. 33 vols. Paris: Cahiers d'Art, 1932–78.

Pollock, Jackson

O'Connor, Francis V. *Jackson Pollock*. New York: The Museum of Modern Art, 1967.

O'Connor, Francis Valentine, and Thaw, Eugene Victor, eds. *Jackson Pollock: A Catalogue Raisonné of Paintings, Drawings, and Other Works*. New Haven: Yale University Press, 1978.

O'Hara, Frank. *Jackson Pollock*. New York: George Braziller, 1959.

Robertson, Bryan, ed. *Jackson Pollock*. New York: Harry N. Abrams, 1960.

Rose, Bernice. *Jackson Pollock: Drawing into Painting*. New York: The Museum of Modern Art, 1980.

Pomodoro, Arnaldo

Bevlin, Marjorie E. *Design Through Discovery*. New York: Holt, Rinehart and Winston, 1977.

Rickey, George

Rosenthal, Nan. *George Rickey*. New York: Harry N. Abrams, 1977.

Riopelle, Jean-Paul

Schneider, Pierre, and Herper, J. Russell. *Jean-Paul Riopelle: Painting and Sculpture*. Ottawa: The National Gallery of Canada, 1962.

Rivera, Diego

New York, The Museum of Modern Art. *Diego Rivera*. 1931.

Rodin, Auguste

Elsen, Albert E. *Rodin*. New York: The Museum of Modern Art, 1963.

Tancock, John L. *The Sculpture of Auguste Rodin*. Philadelphia: The Philadelphia Museum of Art, 1976.

Rosati, James

Waltham, Mass., Brandeis University, Rose Art Museum. *James Rosati: Sculpture 1963 to 1969*. 1969.

Rothko, Mark

Selz, Peter. *Mark Rothko*. New York: The Museum of Modern Art, 1961.

Waldman, Diane. *Mark Rothko, 1903 to 1970: A Retrospective*. New York: The Solomon R. Guggenheim Museum, 1978.

Rouault, Georges

Courthion, Pierre. *Georges Rouault*. New York: Harry N. Abrams, 1962.

Soby, James Thrall. *Georges Rouault: Paintings and Prints*. 3d ed. New York: The Museum of Modern Art, 1937.

Rousseau, Henri

Rich, Daniel Catton. *Henri Rousseau*. New York: The Museum of Modern Art, 1946.

Vallier, Dora. *Henri Rousseau*. New York: Harry N. Abrams, 1964.

Schwitters, Kurt

Schmalenbach, Werner. *Kurt Schwitters*. New York: Harry N. Abrams, 1967.

Segal, George

Van der Marck, Jan. *George Segal*. New York: Harry N. Abrams, 1976.

Seley, Jason

Ithaca, N.Y., Cornell University, Andrew Dickson White Museum of Art. *Jason Seley*. 1965.

Smith, David

Fry, Edward. *David Smith Retrospective Exhibition*. New York: The Solomon R. Guggenheim Museum, 1969.

Krauss, Rosalind E. *The Sculpture of David Smith*. New York: Garland, 1977.

Smith, Tony

Lippard, Lucy. *Tony Smith*. New York: Harry N. Abrams, 1972.

Snelson, Kenneth

Calas, Nicolas and Elena. *Icons and Images of the Sixties*. New York: E. P. Dutton, 1971.

Soulages, Pierre

Juin, Hubert. *Soulages*. New York: Grove Press, 1960.

Stella, Frank

Rubin, William S. *Frank Stella*. New York: The Museum of Modern Art, 1970.

Tobey, Mark

Seitz, William C. *Mark Tobey*. New York: The Museum of Modern Art, 1962.

Tomlin, Bradley Walker

Baur, John I. H. *Bradley Walker Tomlin*. New York: Whitney Museum of American Art, 1957.

Buffalo, N.Y., Albright-Knox Art Gallery. *Bradley Walker Tomlin: A Retrospective View*. 1975.

Vlaminck, Maurice de

Sauvage, Marcel. *Vlaminck, sa vie et son message*. Geneva: Pierre Cailler, 1956.

Warhol, Andy

Coplans, John. *Andy Warhol*. Greenwich, Conn.: New York Graphic Society, 1970.

INDEX

Page numbers in *italics* refer to illustrations.

PHOTO CREDITS

The photographs in this book were taken especially for this publication by Lee Boltin. Existing photographs were used for certain works which were not available to be photographed. With the exception of a few whose photographers are not known, those photographs were taken by the following:

Oliver Baker, 42 bottom

Geoffrey Clements, 32, 42 right top, 45 bottom, 170, 176

Jerome Drown, 151 top

Esto Photographic, Inc., frontispiece, 18

Alexandre Georges, 21 bottom

Glenbow Museum, Calgary, Alberta, 56

Samuel Gottscho, 12

Peter A. Juley & Son, 5, 24, 40 left

David Lustig, 167

James Mathews, 78 top

Luis Medina, 108

Tom Scott, 129

Julius Shulman, 122

Soichi Sunami, 165

David Sutton, 216

Charles Uht, 14, 15, 16, 17, 21 top, 29, 30, 37, 39, 40 right top and bottom, 41, 43, 44 left and right, 45 top, 46 left, 46 right top and bottom, 47, 54 bottom, 67, 69, 72 top and bottom, 73 top, 82, 91, 104 bottom, 112 bottom, 113 top and bottom, 118, 120, 123, 125, 134 top, 135, 164, 173, 174, 199, 201, 202, 204, 209

Malcolm Varon, 171, 200

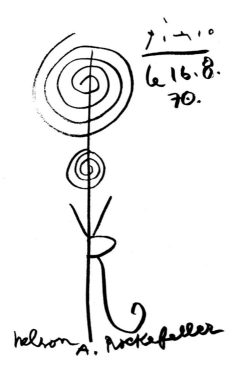

The motif stamped on the front of the binding was drawn in 1970 by Pablo Picasso in orange crayon on the end paper of a copy of the book *El Entierro del Conde de Orgaz* given to Nelson A. Rockefeller.